BALLPARKS
YESTERDAY & TODAY™

Phil Trexler and Marty Strasen

Publications International, Ltd.

Images: Alamy, AP Images, Barry Howe Photography, The Brearley Collection, Corbis, Dreamstime, The Andy Fogel Collection, George Brace Photography, Getty Images, Heritage Auctions, Hunt Auctions, Ted Ingram Collection, Richard A. Johnson Collection, Ron Kuntz, Library of Congress, National Baseball Hall of Fame Library, Cooperstown, N.Y, NewspaperArchive, Susan Pease, Philip Bess and Thursday Associates, SAD Memorabilia, St. Louis Cardinals Hall of Fame Museum, Shutterstock.com, Transcendental Graphics and The Phil Trexler Collection

Photography: Brian Beaugureau Studios; Dan Donovan Photography; Fuchs and Kasperek Photography; Christopher Hiltz; Kelly/Mooney Productions; PDR Productions, Inc.

Written by Phil Trexler and Marty Strasen

Consultant: **Richard A. Johnson**

Factual Verification: **Jake Veyhl**

Yesterday & Today is a trademark of Publications International, Ltd.

Louis Weber, CEO
Publications International, Ltd.
8140 Lehigh Avenue
Morton Grove, Illinois 60053

Permission is never granted for commercial purposes.

ISBN: 978-1-64030-150-4

Manufactured in China.

8 7 6 5 4 3 2 1

CONTENTS

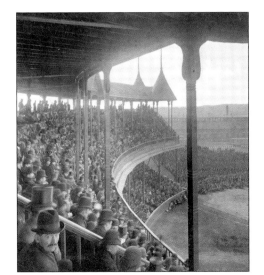

Boston's South End Grounds   Page 9

Tiger Stadium   Page 29

Candlestick Park   Page 62

Chapter 4
THE MODERN AGE 1966–1988   70

RFK Stadium   Page 73

Chapter 5
THE SECOND GOLDEN AGE 1989–TODAY   90

Coors Field   Page 108

Great American Ball Park   Page 124

Chapter 1

EARLY BALLPARKS

1870s–1900

We can close our eyes and still see it, smell it, almost touch it: the wafting tobacco smoke clouding the air, the hecklers, the hawkers, and the crunch-ing of peanut shells under our shoes. Our first ballpark—our second home. From Elysian Fields to the early wooden masterpieces, these grounds helped to shape our understanding of what a ballpark is supposed to be.

Top: Elysian Fields in Hoboken, New Jersey—depicted here in a 19th-century *Harper's Weekly* illustration—served as home to what many consider the first baseball game ever played. *Above:* Produced in small quantities in 1858, this collector's coin commemorated the Pioneer Base Ball Club of Springfield, Massachusetts, one of the first teams to play the game.

VILLAGE GREENS AND ELYSIAN FIELDS

Discovered in an 1861 Princeton College album, this could be the earliest photo of a baseball game in existence. Cricket is being played on the left, baseball on the right.

After shedding the crimson cloak of British imperialism, Americans in the decades that followed went about building a new society. The load was plentiful.

When it came to ball, children still played the imported English games of cricket and rounders. But these games weren't American.

Base, as the earliest version of baseball was named, first appeared in the early 1830s. It was hardly the game we know today. Importantly, it was not English.

The field was square. Players flung balls at advancing runners to record sometimes-bruising outs. Pitchers (called "throwers") intended the ball to be whacked. Baseball was *our* game, from the northern urban neighborhoods to the southern farmlands, and to the vast prairies out west, where Lewis and Clark played a version of the game.

"The game of ball is glorious," noted poet Walt Whitman.

In New York City, the game flourished. By 1845, Alexander Cartwright,

the "Father of Baseball," had incorporated his Knickerbocker Base Ball Club. Cartwright's team played a refined game. The Knickerbockers' field was a diamond, not a square. Bases were 42 paces—or 90 feet—apart. Throws were made to teammates, not at runners. Three outs ended a team's inning. And, finally, baselines established breaks between the action and spectators. These new rules added to the game and to its intrigue.

Across the Hudson River in Hoboken, New Jersey, lies Elysian Fields, with its

The Atlantic Club of Brooklyn and the Mutual Club of New York took to a Big Apple diamond long before such a tussle could be called a "Subway Series."

rolling fields and accessibility to travelers. It was there, on June 19, 1846, that Cartwright organized what many consider to be the first baseball game. The match attracted the curious, but the game was a rout. Cartwright's Knickerbockers were drubbed by the New York Nine, 23–1.

Nevertheless, word quickly spread about this game of baseball. Rich and poor took bats in hand and swiped at balls. Diverse amateur clubs—comprising town laborers, lawyers, doctors, and even undertakers—formed. And people came to watch. America's astute businessmen took notice, wondering aloud if these eager onlookers would actually pay for the privilege. New York would serve as the template.

With the birth in 1857 of the National Association of Base Ball Players (NABBP) came the sport's first rivalry: New York against Brooklyn. It was, in a sense, a premonition of the Giants–Dodgers feud. Street-corner arguments

rose over which was the better team. The score was settled on July 20, 1858, in what is considered the first paid-admission baseball game.

The game's site, Fashion Race Course, was more noted for dashing ponies than lazy pop-ups, but it proved to be a suitable spot for the New York–Brooklyn battle. Players arrived that afternoon in triumphantly grand style, escorted in garish horse-drawn vehicles. Many fans circled the converted track after spending hard-earned currency to hitch two-horse coaches. The game was an all-star matchup of the best from Manhattan and Hoboken against the prime players from Brooklyn's four squads. The New Yorkers rallied late to win, 22–18.

By 1862, baseball had found its original field of dreams. Businessman William Cammeyer partitioned his failing Brooklyn ice-skating rink with a six-foot wooden fence, creating what historians consider America's first enclosed ballpark, the Union Base Ball

and Cricket Grounds. Unemployed workers executed the transformation and the task of leveling and sodding the six-acre plot.

As many as 1,500 spectators were offered—free of charge at this first game—seats in the horseshoe-shape grandstand. Flags of NABBP clubs flapped in the summer air atop staffs. Players were given an expansive clubhouse that was large enough to accommodate three teams. The park was embraced—hundreds gathered inside, while more stood and rung the outfield some 500 feet from home plate. These crowds would watch rival NABBP clubs such as the Brooklyn Eckfords and the New York Mutuals.

Gamblers and rascals were segregated inside, as Union Grounds was billed a "suitable place for ball playing, where ladies can witness the game without being annoyed by the indecorous behavior of the rowdies." Ten-cent admissions were gladly paid, as throngs of people regularly gathered to take in the exciting new sport.

America's game was becoming its national pastime.

Knickerbocker Base Ball Club founder Alexander Cartwright is considered the "Father of Baseball" for passing down a version of the game that would skyrocket in popularity.

BALLYARDS OF THE NATIONAL ASSOCIATION

Top: The impressive grandstand of the original Sportsman's Park was located on the southeast corner of its rural St. Louis block to allow fans easy access from North Grand Avenue. *Above:* Baseball was played in the original Sportsman's Park as far back as 1867. The Brown Stockings were a big draw during the venue's early years.

In the 1860s, soldiers in the Civil War learned to play baseball. After the war, these soldiers returned to their homes and helped to spread the sport's popularity. Baseball would help stitch a nation's wounds.

Baseball, for a time, was an amateur's game. Paying for play was thought to be uncivilized. But competition wiped away that pretense of civility. The National Association of Base Ball Players, supposedly an amateur league, learned that its players were reaping financial benefits: gate shares, salaries, and even sundry profits. In response, nine clubs rushed to form the National Association of Professional Base Ball Players (the "NA") in 1871, with franchises in Boston; Chicago; Cleveland; Fort Wayne, Indiana; New York; Philadelphia; Rockford, Illinois; Troy, New York; and Washington, D.C.

This new league would blaze a bumpy trail over its brief lifespan. Nevertheless, major-league baseball was born. And ballparks were needed—fast. Within two months of the league's founding, owners signed players, set schedules and rules, and crafted enclosed parks in which they would seat paying customers. Wood, which was easily accessible, was the favored construction material, and ballparks rose up wherever affordable city space permitted.

The NA's crown jewel was Hamilton Field, home of the Fort Wayne Kekiongas. Dubbed the "Grand Duchess" by city loyalists for its ornate grandstand, the park hosted the first major-league game, on May 4, 1871. Rain limited the crowd to 200, but Fort Wayne hurler Bobby Mathews kept Cleveland bats flailing in a 2–0 win. Two months later, the Duchess was shuttered due to a lack of money.

In Chicago, the White Stockings played at Union Base-Ball Grounds (also known as "Lake Park"), which was built on a landfill near Lake Michigan. A season ticket cost $15, and Union

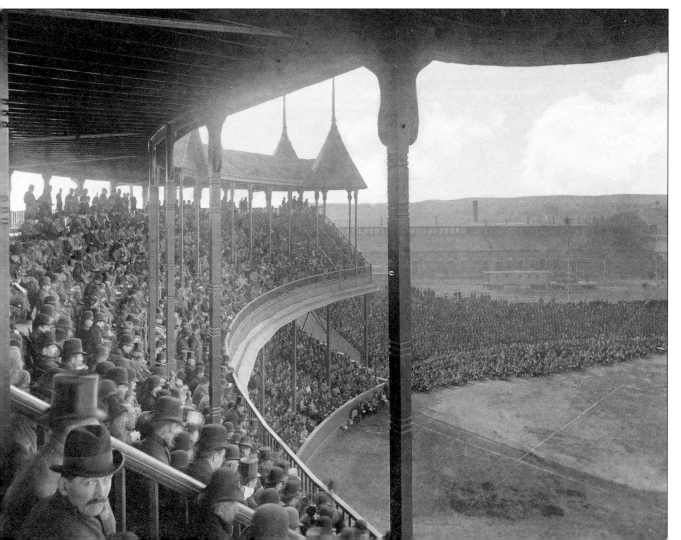

The second incarnation of Boston's South End Grounds was sometimes called the "Grand Pavilion," a reference to the 1888 Walpole Street jewel's magnificent double-deck grandstand.

Grounds could hold 7,000 spectators. Men and women were given separate accommodations. The outfield was sprawling—its center-field wall was 375 feet from home plate. But in October 1871, as swiftly as a cow's kick, the devastating Great Chicago Fire erupted. The blaze swept through the city, engulfing the ballpark—and the Stockings' pennant chances that first season.

Sportsman's Park in St. Louis was born in the NA prior to the league's final season. The stadium's rural setting would serve as the city's baseball centerpiece for nearly a century. Originally called the Grand Avenue Ball Grounds, the 800-seat park was home to the city's Brown Stockings for the 1875 season. Fans gushed over the surroundings.

Athletics Park in Philadelphia boasted the first press box. In 1871, it saw the A's take the NA's first-ever championship. Haymakers' Grounds, which was located near the Hudson River in Troy, offered a covered grandstand and little else; its tenants, the Troy Haymakers, folded midway through the '72 season "on account of an empty treasury."

Fairgrounds Park in Rockford was literally fashioned inside a fairground, with trees dotting the third-base line; it was fitting for a team called the Forest Citys. They went a woeful 1–17 away from the park and folded before the 1871 season ended.

One NA survivor was New York's entry, the Mutuals, which played at Union Grounds in Brooklyn. Distance didn't thwart 3,000 fans from attending the Mutuals' opener against Troy. But an unexpected hike in tickets prices from the year before—from two bits to four—sent many a New Yorker grumbling home.

In Boston, the Red Stockings made sure Beantown would never go another season without a professional team after player/manager Harry Wright's team took to the South End Grounds in 1871. "Baseball is business now," Wright said. He knew a thing or two about paying ballplayers—he recruited baseball's first pro team, the almost-unbeatable 1869 Cincinnati Red Stockings. Many of that team's prized players followed Wright to New England.

South End Grounds was a no-frills, no-grass ball field. Walpole Street was located just beyond a rickety four-row set of box seats, and bleachers extended down the first-base line. Signs urged patrons to buy soda from licensed vendors. With Wright at the helm and backed by a generous budget, Boston's success was plentiful.

Alas, the Red Stockings' sheer domi-nance—buoyed by Al Spalding, the league's finest pitcher—would hasten the imbalanced league's demise. Boston won four of the NA's five titles and posted an unfathomable 71–8 mark in 1875. The club drew 70,000 fans that season, the league's last.

MASTERPIECES IN WOOD

By the 1890s, America was thriving, and despite a mid-decade stock-market collapse, baseball continued its climb. Its parks, while crude by today's standards, served as the sport's marquee, just as baseball pioneer Harry Wright envisioned.

"We must make the games worth witnessing and there will be no fault found with the price of admission," he opined. "A good game is worth 50 cents. A poor one is dear at 25."

As the National League (which had risen from the ashes of the National Association in 1876) shrugged off challenges from the fledgling Players League and the flailing American Association, new ballparks were crammed inside urban neighborhoods all around the eastern region. Some disappeared unexpectedly, as fire ravaged as many as 21 all-wood ballparks during the decade.

Four NL parks went up in flames in 1894

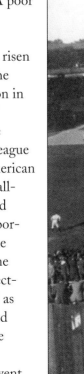

Above: The Boston Beaneaters pose in front of the new Grand Pavilion in 1888, the first year after the South End Grounds were renovated. *Right:* Nickel admission, a beer garden, and winning baseball brought fans out in droves to Union Park in Baltimore. Here, the Orioles defeat the Boston Beaneaters to win the 1897 Temple Cup (a short-lived National League championship).

alone. But perhaps the greatest loss was that of the lavish South End Grounds in Boston. Marked by six majestic turrets that towered over a double-deck Grand Pavilion, it had served as the Beaneaters' home since a renovation of its predecessor after the 1887 season.

The Boston lineup packed a wallop, as attested by its five pennants in seven seasons. But alas, tight-fisted team owner Arthur Soden grossly underinsured his ballpark. His cheapness (he once forced players' wives to buy tickets) bit him in his pocketbook during a game against

Baltimore when, according to one story, a wayward cigarette touched off flames, and the Grand Pavilion was toast. A less-grand park was slapped together in a mere ten weeks.

The era's most enduring park was the third incarnation of Manhattan's Polo Grounds, a stadium that would host New York's Giants—and baseball history—for more than six decades. The horseshoe-shape park opened in 1891. With its home plate nestled under Coogan's Bluff, the park offered amenities that befitted New Yorkers: fine sight

The Winning Game of 1897 Boston vs Baltimore.

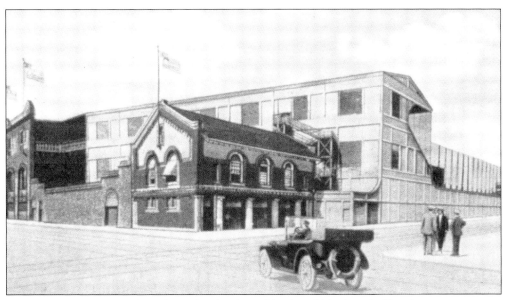

League Park was jammed inside a Cleveland neighborhood block and offered easy access to games. It served as home to the Spiders of the National League, the Indians of the American League, and the Cleveland Buckeyes of the Negro American League.

lines, divine food, and choice liquor from a bar with a view under the grandstand. The bluff itself also provided free seats to the less well-off. Across the city, along Jamaica Bay, sat Brooklyn's Eastern Park, the home of the Brooklyn Bridegrooms. Fans often dodged trolleys on their way inside, which gave rise to the team's future nickname.

In Baltimore, a nickel allowed fans access to Union Park. Awaiting them inside were picnic tables and a beer garden, where fans could soak in the sun and suds. The field was specially groomed for the Orioles and their brand of "Little Ball," which brought them three straight NL championships from 1894 to 1896. Stars like Wee Willie Keeler took full advantage of the hard infield, where a smash into the clay dirt shot the ball into a "Baltimore Chop."

National League Park, the forerunner to Philadelphia's infamous Baker Bowl, was a palatial engineering marvel after it was rebuilt following an 1894 fire. With its imposing medieval exterior, the park was the first to incorporate concrete and brick into its grandstand. Thanks to cantilevers, obstructing support columns vanished.

Ohio was home to two fields with the same name: League Park, in Cleveland and Cincinnati. Like many fields of the day, Cleveland's park was located along its owner's trolley line and was awkwardly squeezed inside a neighborhood block. Cincinnati's version seemed cursed from Opening Day 1884, when a section of the grandstand collapsed, killing one. Reds fans returned in droves, however, and the club often outdrew teams from larger cities.

LUXURY ON THE LAKEFRONT

It was, recalls baseball historian Michael Benson, "the finest park of the era."

Lake Front Park in Chicago was indeed fit for a king: Albert Spalding, the Hall of Fame hurler, sporting goods magnate, and owner of the Chicago White Stockings. Lake Front Park—which was built near the site of Union Grounds, its fire-ravaged predecessor—grew with its team's fortunes, eventually offering unheard-of amenities.

Following an 1882 NL championship, Spalding went on a spending binge. Outside the park, an ornate pagoda ushered fans through the main gate, where 41 eager workers waited to please. The grandstand was expanded and the park grew to seat 10,000. Above the third base stands sat Spalding's cash cow—18 luxury boxes, which offered padded armchairs and privacy curtains for Chicago's elite. A telephone (then a new gadget), was installed in Spalding's private box. Bleacher seats jutted into right field, creating a 196-foot home-run porch, which Chicago sluggers often targeted. (The following year, those balls were, by league rule, ground-rule doubles.)

Spalding's kingdom crumbled after three seasons, however. Lake Front Park, it was learned, was built on federal land, on which businesses were banned.

This 1880s postcard depicts Lake Front Park. Note the left inset, which pictures a luxury box.

Chapter 2

THE GOLDEN AGE

1901–1932

As the 20th century dawned, baseball was becoming ingrained in the hearts of Americans, who were laboring in an industrial age and in search of distractions from their daily toils. Refuge came in baseball. Alas, major-league ballparks remained in the dark ages—they were wooden, rickety, and sometimes perilous. That was all about to change.

Above: This terra-cotta "spider-style" catcher's mask once adorned the outside of the grandstand at the original Yankee Stadium. It was removed during renovations to the park in the 1970s. *Right:* Lights now shine at Chicago's Wrigley Field, the last of the night-baseball holdouts, but the park retains its early-20th-century charm for the faithful fans on the North Side.

THE POLO GROUNDS: COOGAN'S BLUFF

Down a set of stairs from the ledge of Coogan's Bluff awaits a ticket booth to history—some of baseball's grandest and darkest events occurred on this site. It is here that the world heard Bobby Thomson's shot, Willie Mays made "The Catch," and Cleveland's Ray Chapman died after being hit by a pitch.

For the first part of the 20th century, John McGraw and his New York Giants dominated baseball. Their home was the Polo Grounds, a classic venue with a snappy name that was favored by New Yorkers who followed the park over several rebuilds and locations, as well as one devastating fire that blazed early in the 1911 season.

The "Polo Grounds" moniker was introduced in the 1880s to describe a site near Central Park where polo had once been played. But it was alongside Coogan's Bluff (which was named after its longtime landowner) that baseball and the Polo Grounds were forever linked. Three parks were built under the bluff, but the most enduring and historic Polo Grounds opened on June 28, 1911, and served as the Giants' home for the next four-and-a-half decades. It would be, as owner John Brush envisioned, "a model for all subsequent base ball structures."

Brush, a Civil War vet and clothing store magnate, showered lavishness all over his new steel-and-concrete ballpark.

His Giants, managed by the tyrannical McGraw, responded with three straight pennants. The bathtub-shape park, which was contoured to fit inside the bluff, was indeed a treasure, but the structure blocked the view from onlookers who once sat atop Coogan's Bluff for a distant—yet free—show.

With its frescoes of the Roman Coliseum's facade, the park held unique amenities, such as a staircase that took fans from the bluff's peak to a ticket booth that sat behind home plate. Other ornate subtleties included the coat of arms of each National League team adorning the grandstand roof. The playing field was equally unique, with

Before outfield bleachers blocked the view, fans could park their horses and carriages or stand behind ropes in the outfield to watch games at the Polo Grounds.

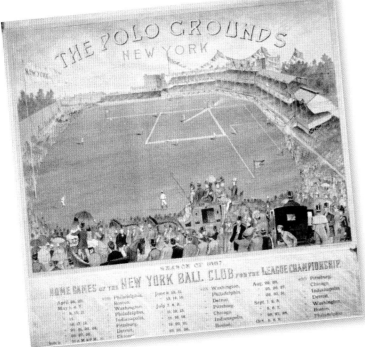

The Polo Grounds New York

Above: A double-deck grandstand that stretched down the baselines, bleacher seats in the outfield, and a gargantuan area for center fielders to patrol were staples of the old park at Coogan's Bluff.
Right: Willie Mays was a favorite at the Polo Grounds, first as a New York Giants star and later when he returned with San Francisco to face the Mets there in 1962.

short fences in right and left fields and a mammoth 500-foot pasture in center. In time, an overhanging upper deck made a left-field homer even more appetizing.

The stadium's seating capacity grew over time, from 16,000 to more than 56,000, as the double-deck grandstand was stretched to both foul poles. Single-deck bleachers held firm in center, separated by a five-story structure that held the team offices, team club-houses, and a scoreboard. Beginning in 1913, the Polo Grounds was also home to the American League's Yankees, a team that shook the baseball world after it acquired a power-hitting former

pitcher named Babe Ruth in 1920. In McGraw's house, the Yankees became the first team to draw one million fans, which they accomplished each year in the Polo Grounds from 1920 to 1922.

With the Sultan of Swat hammering away at the Polo Grounds' short right-field porch, the stadium's two tenants met in the World Series in 1921 and 1922; the Giants won both champion-ships. The Yankees' success at the gate and in the standings brought with them an eviction notice. Ruth and his mates would find a new home in the Bronx.

"I cried when they took me out of the Polo Grounds," Ruth moped. After the 1957 season, Giant fans cried too—their team moved from the Polo Grounds to San Francisco, joining the Dodgers in vacating New York for California.

WORKING FOR PEANUTS

Guys like Babe Ruth see a hot dog and just take a bite. Harry M. Stevens saw one and decided to become the "King of Sports Concessions."

Stevens's story is nearly as mythical as Abner Doubleday's. Legend once credited Stevens with inventing hot dogs at the Polo Grounds in 1905, but research has debunked the tale. What Stevens did first, and very well, was *market* hot dogs—as well as scorecards and other ballpark concessions— creating a profitable business inside a business.

His empire started in Ohio with scorecards he sold at amateur

This 1920s hot dog vending steamer is made of solid copper.

fields. "I had to convince [fans] that a game could not be really enjoyed without a scorecard," he said. Stevens saw handsome profits, one dime at a time. He soon took his business to New York, where he expanded his company to sell hot dogs and other concessions. In 1994, concession giant ARAMARK bought Stevens's company for $150 million.

THE BAKER BOWL "HUMP"

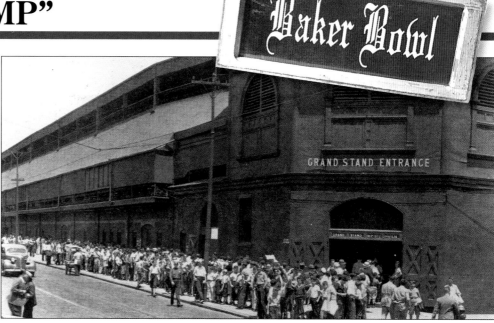

On the north end of Philadelphia she sat, "Hump" and all. To paraphrase baseball writer Red Smith, the Baker Bowl had all the charm of a city dump; all it lacked was the size.

Indeed, the Baker Bowl was a hitter's park. Phillies slugger Chuck Klein routinely banged shots off and over the 60-foot right-field wall, which was plastered with a Lifebuoy soap ad. Despite this monument to cleanliness, harsh Philadelphia fans reminded everyone, "The Phillies still stink."

It wasn't always odorous in this ballpark. When it was rebuilt after an 1894 fire, the Bowl—which was named for Phillies owner William Baker—was viewed as an engineering marvel. It had a double-deck grandstand made of steel, brick, and concrete—a baseball first. The cantilevered design meant that there were no obstructive poles. Despite the upgrades, the flimsiness of the ballpark's wooden

The Baker Bowl featured short porches in all fields but center. Even during the dead-ball era, hitters routinely knocked home runs the mere 280 or 300 feet they needed to travel to clear these walls.

Top: This old wooden transom sat over a door at Philadelphia's Baker Bowl in the early 1900s. The stadium hosted the 1915 World Series between the Red Sox and Phillies. *Bottom:* Formally, it was known as "National League Park." But Philadelphians who came out to watch games at the corner of Broad and Huntingdon streets called it the "Baker Bowl."

bleachers along left field led to disaster during a game in 1903; twelve fans died when the section collapsed.

The park enforced stern rules proscribing "temperance, order and discipline." Sunday ballgames were outlawed. Winning ballgames also seemed to be anathema, as the Phillies held fast to the National League's second division, winning just a single NL pennant during the more than 50 summers they spent in the stadium.

The Baker Bowl was a bandbox, with seating for fewer than 20,000 and a right-field wall that stood just 280 feet from home plate and shot balls back into the field in all directions. This intimacy gave rise to another Smith quip—he joked that the wall was so close to the

infield that a second baseman could tell if the right fielder had eaten onions.

In center field stood the team's clubhouse, rising 35 feet and offering a dozen windows that the great Cardinals second baseman Rogers Hornsby once successfully targeted. In front of this structure was the "Hump," a grassy bump in deep center that reminded all of what was below: a Philadelphia and Reading Railroad tunnel. For a time, sheep grazed at the Bowl, trimming the grass. The once-grand ballpark became a Philadelphia punch line as it aged—thrifty ownership, poor attendance, and consistent losing provided for few reinvestment opportunities. The Phillies left the Bowl for beautiful Shibe Park during the 1938 season.

SHIBE PARK EMERGES IN CONCRETE

For too long, fire proved to be baseball's most formidable foe. Rickety wooden grandstands provided no-frills intimacy for clamoring fans—but also kindling for flames. Shortly after the turn of the century, thinking changed in Philadelphia, where Shibe Park—made of sturdy steel and concrete—emerged along Lehigh Avenue and 21st Street.

The home of the Athletics, Shibe was named for the team's primary owner, Ben Shibe. It presented comfort and grace by 1909 standards. Its exterior facade anchored a French Renaissance tower with rows of arched windows and scrolled columns. It was designed and built by the firm of William Steele and Sons (ironically enough). And while there had been some ballparks that had integrated concrete or steel-reinforced concrete into mostly wood structures, Shibe was the first that arose using a steel-and-concrete frame. The club's willingness to spend a great deal more

money on a ballpark that used steel and concrete rather than less-expensive wood also signaled a change in baseball economics. Franchises were putting down roots in communities, and there was greater stability in professional baseball than there had been in the past.

Inside of Shibe, a double-deck grandstand cradled the infield. Bleacher seating along the third-base side jutted sharply from left to center field, creating an imposing 515-foot cavern from home plate to center field. With no seating beyond right field, the park was an inviting sight to fans perched on neighboring rooftops. (In later years, after a failed lawsuit by the A's, a "spite fence" that blocked the free view was built.)

Seating was initially offered for 20,000, but thousands more crammed inside after Shibe's gates opened on April 12, 1909. The A's, piloted by manager Connie Mack, beat the Boston Red Sox, 8–1.

"It was a great day for Philadelphia in the baseball world. It was a great day for the fans," hailed the *Philadelphia Bulletin*.

Immediate success ensued at Shibe Park—the A's, led by hitting greats Home Run Baker and Eddie Collins, won four pennants and three World Series crowns from 1910 to 1914. Shibe Park, which was renamed in Mack's honor in 1953, proved itself hardy over six decades, especially considering its original $455,000 price tag. From 1938 to 1954, it housed more than one team.

Above: Fans who lived on a stretch of 20th Street behind Philadelphia's Shibe Park enjoyed a unique perk: free views of games from their rooftop perches. *Below:* Greats like Richie Ashburn, Robin Roberts, and George Kell are among those who etched their names into Shibe Park's history.

HUNTINGTON GROUNDS JUST ACROSS TRACKS

Right: A record crowd of nearly 34,000, including several seated on a Bull Durham tobacco sign, saw Boston play Detroit at Huntington Avenue Grounds on August 9, 1911. *Below:* With an upward-sloping field leading to fences that stood a country-mile from home plate, overflow crowds could safely stand in the outfield at Boston's pitcher-friendly Huntington Avenue Grounds.

Few remember that the Boston Red Sox played anywhere other than Fenway Park. Forgotten by many fans is Huntington Avenue Grounds, the Sox's first American League home.

Huntington Avenue Grounds housed the Sox—who were known as the Americans until 1908—as the start-up AL opened in 1901, thanks to some arm-twisting by league founder Ban Johnson, who persuaded Charles Somers to finance a team for the city. Somers had just weeks and $35,000 with which to build his ballpark. "We shall have accommodations that will please everyone interested, from the 'fresh candy' man to the members of the 400," Somers declared.

Built on the site of an old circus near a railroad yard, Huntington Grounds was directly across the tracks from the South End Grounds—the home field of Boston's National League ball club. It was one of the first guerilla sports-marketing strikes in American business history.

Huntington Grounds sat 9,000, though twice as many could stand inside. The stone, steel, and wood grandstand was easy to enter: There was one gate and one turnstile. Inside, affluent fans were offered opera chairs; the less fortunate sat on wood bleachers.

It may have been baseball's oddest ballpark. The field was like the game back then: rough-and-tumble. Splotches of sand abated grass, and the landscape sloped upward in a spacious center field, where overflowing crowds could safely stand. Some estimate the fences in center field were more than 500 feet from batters, a homer in left field needed 350 feet, and a comparatively meager 280-foot drive could clear the wall in right.

In the dead-ball era, the park suited Boston pitching

stalwart Cy Young, who tossed the first game in the stadium in 1901 and, two years later, carried the Americans to the World Series, where they topped the Pittsburgh Pirates to win the franchise's first championship. The next season, Young twirled the era's first perfect game. Fenway Park owes Huntington for one thing: When Huntington closed after the 1911 season, parts of its infield sod were moved to the Red Sox's new home. A plaque and a statue of Cy Young mark the area now on Northeastern University where Huntington Grounds once stood.

THE HIGHLANDERS HIT NEW YORK'S HILLTOP PARK

Those who sought to keep the fledgling American League out of the bustling metropolis of New York underestimated the business acumen of AL President Ban Johnson. Wheeling, dealing, and plenty of political palm-greasing at Tammany Hall helped lay the foundation of what was to become baseball's greatest dynasty—the New York Yankees.

Andrew Freedman—the owner of the National League's New York Giants—thought he had gobbled up enough prime real estate (and politicians) to keep any commercial threats to his club at bay. He was wrong. Johnson and a syndicate—including political insider Joseph Gordon, pool-hall owner Frank Farrell, and Chief of Police William Devery—planted their franchise in a run-down section of Washington Heights on a rock pile at Hilltop Park. Rapidly raised, single-deck, and absolutely no-frills, the park alongside Broadway and 165th Street was able to seat 16,000 fans; its standing room could almost double that number.

The Orioles relocated from Baltimore, were renamed the Highlanders, and opened Hilltop Park in April 1903. Fans at the spartan stadium could take in an elevated view of the Hudson River and the New Jersey Palisades from Manhattan Island's tallest peak. Originally called American League Park, it was built in six weeks for $75,000 and featured a sloping outfield that sometimes left a swamp for right fielders.

Opening Day was a sellout; fans waved tiny American flags, and the 69th

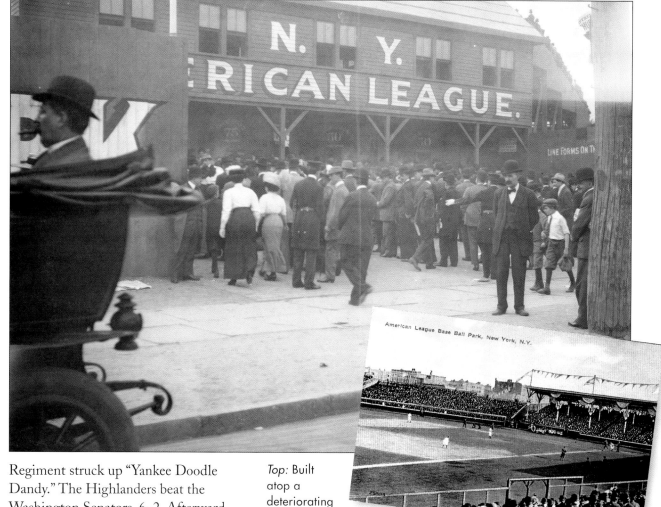

American League Base Ball Park, New York, N.Y.

Regiment struck up "Yankee Doodle Dandy." The Highlanders beat the Washington Senators, 6–2. Afterward, fans exited through a gate in right field. Players had to change in a hotel until a center-field clubhouse was ready.

Hilltop Park remained unchanged through its life, and the Highlanders' ownership's rivalry with the Giants waned. In fact, the Giants called Hilltop their home for a spell after a 1911 fire gutted the Polo Grounds. Beginning in 1912, the Giants returned the favor—

Top: Built atop a deteriorating section of Manhattan's Washington Heights neighborhood and opened in 1903, Hilltop Park seated 16,000 fans and offered standing room for another 10,000. *Bottom:* Long before they were known as the Yankees, the New York Highlanders played at no-frills Hilltop Park, a pitcher's paradise with a spacious outfield.

they shared the rebuilt Polo Grounds with the newly rechristened Yankees, who abandoned Hilltop and stayed in Manhattan for a decade.

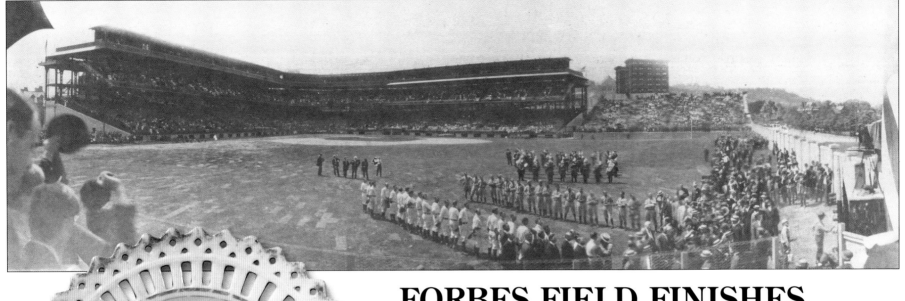

Top: Fans viewing games from the furthest reaches of Forbes Field had to fix their eyes more than 460 feet for glimpses of batters or plays at home plate. *Above:* This 100-year-old porcelain souvenir dish pays tribute to Forbes Field. The Pittsburgh stadium served up triples galore, though home runs were difficult to come by.

FORBES FIELD FINISHES "FOLLY" FOLDEROL

Some folly.

After Barney Dreyfuss's construction crew put the final touches on Forbes Field, those pundits who dared question the new home for his Pittsburgh Pirates were left speechless. When Forbes Field opened in 1909, it was a palace of modern proportions. It offered convenience and comfort, and was a royal blueprint that other teams followed. With accommodations for 25,000, it was the largest park in baseball. It proved suitable for Dreyfuss's Pirates when it opened, who won a hotly contested World Series against Ty Cobb and the Detroit Tigers that first fall.

"It's impossible to properly describe Forbes Field," a writer for *The Sporting News* gushed.

Critics panned the park for its grandeur, immense size, and distance from the city's downtown, dubbing it "Dreyfuss's Folly." But it was worth the trip. Forbes Field—which was named after British war hero Brigadier General John Forbes—erased all memories of Exposition Park, an outdated wood facility along the Allegheny River that had hosted Pirates baseball for nearly 20 years. "The game was growing up, and patrons were no longer willing to put up with nineteenth-century conditions," Dreyfuss said.

The Pirates' new double-deck abode, built of concrete and steel for $2 million, offered ramps and elevators instead of stairs. It had restrooms in the upper deck, where maids attended more affluent fans. Dreyfuss also provided public telephones—his idea was to include the masses, from wealthy bankers to struggling steelworkers. Specialty box seats for eight could be purchased for $10; a bleacher seat could be had for a quarter. Streetcars eased the three-mile jaunt for inner-city fans, some of whom showed up six hours early for Opening Day 1909.

This supposed folly of a park drew more than 30,000 that first afternoon for a contest with the defending National League champs, the Chicago Cubs. While the Pirates lost that game, they went on to win 110 games and claim the NL pennant, thanks in large part to their storied shortstop, Honus Wagner. In the World Series, Wagner ignored the taunts of Cobb and staked his claim to being the game's greatest player as he led the Pirates to the championship.

One ballpark attraction Dreyfuss resisted was cheap home runs. Forbes Field was a park for rapping triples—not dingers—thanks to fences 360 feet down the left-field line, 462 to center, and 376 to right. Bucs outfielder John "Chief" Wilson took advantage of the dimensions, smacking a record 36 triples in 1912. Yet despite its expansive outfield, no team was ever held hitless in more than 4,000 games at Forbes.

The stadium saw only minor changes during its more than 60 seasons as the Pirates' home turf. Seating was expanded several times, its fences were eventually drawn in, and, in 1947, an ivy-covered brick wall went up near an imposing scoreboard in left field. Over its life span, the park played host to history: a Pirates World Series win in 1925, the prowess of slugging outfielder Ralph Kiner, the prime seasons of Roberto Clemente's career, and the unforgettable World Series-winning home run from light-hitting second baseman Bill Mazeroski in 1960. On June 28, 1970, nearly 41,000 fans turned out to bid farewell to the enduring folly.

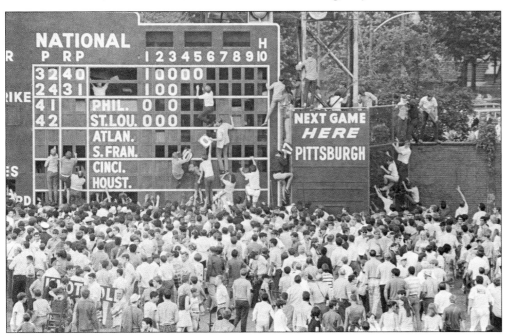

THE BAMBINO BIDS ADIEU

HE WAS AN American idol, but Babe Ruth was well past his prime when he joined the Boston Braves in 1935.

Braves Field seemed to be starving for attention when Ruth, who had been released by the Yankees, was lured to Boston to be player/vice president/assistant manager. Braves owner Emil Fuchs assured Ruth that he would manage the club in 1936. It was all a ruse.

Ruth started his Braves career with a bang, clubbing a homer before a sold-out Opening Day crowd. Ever the showman, Ruth mustered another legendary performance in Pittsburgh on May 25, when he smacked three homers, the last of which—career dinger 714—he called himself. "He pointed to a group of old guys clapping for him and said he'd put it over the roof," recalled witness Paul Warhola, brother of renowned artist Andy Warhol.

Hitting .181 and realizing that Fuchs's promises were false, Ruth retired five days later.

Fans scaled the scoreboard for keepsakes after the final game played at Forbes Field, the nightcap of a June 1970 doubleheader between the Pirates and Chicago Cubs.

SOUTH SIDE PARK CREATES "HITLESS WONDERS"

It was, without question, the deadest of the dead-ball-era parks. Chicago's South Side Park—residence to the White Sox as the American League was born in 1901—housed the "Hitless Wonders" and propelled pitcher Ed Walsh into baseball immortality.

South Side Park was the third ballpark erected in the Armour Square neighborhood in the city's southern end, where

the Chicago Cricket Club first opened in the 1880s. Many grumbled about the remote location, but a train line that connected the stadium to downtown eased the commute, much to the satisfaction of Sox owner Charles Comiskey. The park hosted the American League's first game, between the Sox and the Cleveland Blues, on April 24, 1901.

While its giant single-deck wood grandstands—which were propped up by stilt-like supports to improve sight lines—could hold 15,000 fans, South Side Park's outfield seemed like an unending pasture, its limits unreachable by even the most powerful hitters of the era. Its dimensions are subject to debate, but the corner fences are known to have been longer than those in center field.

Some seasons, no homers were hit there; other years, there were two, three, or four.

This suited Sox pitchers such as Walsh—a lanky right-hander who packed a slippery spitball—just fine. Twice that decade, the Sox won pennants; in 1906, they captured the World Series against the crosstown-rival Cubs. But a 1909 fire that gutted the grandstands coupled with the wild popularity of the White Sox doomed South Side Park. Comiskey built a grander park in his own name; it opened during the 1910 season.

South Side Park continued to host baseball for another 30 years, thanks in large part to Negro National League founder Rube Foster and his partner John M. Schorling, who was a saloonkeeper and Comiskey's son-in-law. The stadium became home to several of Negro League teams. It was at South Side Park that Foster worked as a manager, owner, and baseball trailblazer. Chicago's Negro League entries dominated their competition in the 1920s, winning three pennants and two championships during the decade. The venue's run ended in 1940 when a Christmas Day fire brought the long-standing wood park down.

Top: Scoreboard operators at South Side Park hung a couple of big numbers on this day, but a typical afternoon there featured plenty of zeroes at this pitcher's dream. *Left:* South Side Park hosted big crowds when the Cubs and White Sox staged a City Championship Series in October 1909. The Cubs prevailed, four games to one.

WHITE SOX vs CUBS
CITY CHAMPIONSHIP SERIES
Chicago, Oct. 10, '09 West Side Park.

WEST SIDE PARK SEES CUBS WIN TITLE

It was the grass-and-dirt playground of Tinker to Evers to Chance, a rickety wood ballpark whose history is almost lost in the shadow of its celebrated successor. But West Side Park in Chicago saw something that Wrigley Field had to wait until 2016 to witness: a World Series championship team.

In the early 1900s, the ballpark at Polk and South Wood streets hosted one of the National League's most successful franchises, which was led by the afore-mentioned poetic double-play combination. And during its 22-year span as home to the Cubs, West Side Park saw its share of triumphs, challenges, and, of course, rooftop wars that pitted neighbors seeking freebies against club owners looking to sell tickets.

The Cubs played in the World Series four times from 1906 to 1910. Led by pitching ace Mordecai "Three Finger" Brown, the Cubs won a pair of championship titles, but never did they celebrate the final out before their home fans. It took more than a century for Cubs fans to enjoy an encore.

The Cubs were called the Colts when the second West Side Park (the first was abandoned by the team in 1891) opened in 1893. The next season, one-third of all major-league ballparks were struck by fires; Chicago's happened in the seventh inning of an August contest. Colt players Jimmy Ryan and Walt Wilmot won acclaim for creating an escape route for some 1,600 stampeding fans who fled the burning grandstand for the field.

Still, at least 100 were injured. The team played at the park the next day.

Like many urban ballparks, West Side Park was crammed inside a dense neighborhood, which gave it a rectangular shape and asymmetrical dimensions, including a whopping 560 feet to center field. Located two miles from downtown and near an "L" train stop, the ballpark could seat 16,000, but hundreds chose to stand on the outfield's outer limits. That expansive pasture served Philadelphia slugger Ed Delahanty well during an 1896 game in which he smacked a record four homers, not one of which went over the fence.

Top: Inside-the-park home runs were not uncommon at West Side Park, where Cubs players and their opponents had to launch balls well over 500 feet to clear parts of the fence. *Above:* The last time the Cubs won a World Series, it was the wood stands of West Side Park that held their fans. The stadium hosted four World Series from 1906 to 1910.

COMISKEY: "BASEBALL PALACE OF THE WORLD"

Only Charles "Commy" Comiskey could take an abandoned city dump, combine it with the ripe smell of a stockyard, and craft his self-titled "Baseball Palace of the World." But there it stood on the Chicago's South Side—a venerable ballpark adored by generations of White Sox fans.

Comiskey had two loves vying for his attention: winning and money. The Sox of the early 1900s brought him on-field success—two pennants and a World Series title—but the antiquated confines of South Side Park no longer suited Commy's empirical taste.

On St. Patrick's Day 1910, Comiskey laid his foundation—a green cornerstone squeezed in place, marking the occasion— atop an old dump near the corner of South Shields Avenue and 35th Street. Less than four months later, as a brass band sounded "Hail to the Chief," Comiskey Park flung open its gates, unveiling a sun-splashed open-arch concourse and a bunting-draped grandstand. "Few ball fields have gotten off to so unabashedly sentimental a start as Comiskey Park," wrote historian Michael Gershman.

Comiskey's palace could have been grander. Original plans called for a decorative Romanesque facade and a cantilevered upper deck. But Comiskey held his pocketbook close, keeping the stadium's cost at just over $700,000. The park sat 32,000, and Comiskey, ever mindful of Chicago's working class, provided 7,000 of those seats for a mere quarter each, which routinely pushed the Sox's attendance near the top of the American League. The outfield, with its closest fence 362 feet away from home plate, was spacious by design, since Sox ace Ed Walsh helped vet the park's plans. Ironically, Walsh was on the losing end of the stadium's first game, a 2–0 affair against the lowly St. Louis Browns.

As seasons went on, Commy's Sox improved. They won two pennants in the late teens, the second of which was marred by the "Black Sox" scandal of 1919, which sent the franchise into a

The lineup cards from the inaugural Major League Baseball All-Star Game—which was held at Comiskey Park on July 6, 1933—read like a Hall of Fame roster.

With a pitcher, Ed Walsh, influencing its design, it's no wonder Comiskey opened with pitcher-friendly dimensions. The fences eventually moved in, but the park rarely favored hitters.

Not even circumstances like the 1919 "Black Sox" scandal and the Great Depression of the 1930s could keep Chicagoans from coming out to Comiskey Park.

40-year spiral. In 1927, four years before Commy's death, 20,000 seats were added via an expanded upper deck and bleacher section. This extra seating came in handy when Comiskey hosted baseball's first All-Star Game in 1933. Walsh's prized expansive outfield inhaled and exhaled during the 1940s, depending on the Sox's opponents' hitting prowess and the whims of General Manager Frank Lane. For a time, white garden hoses were flattened to serve as foul lines.

It took the circus-like sales pitches of Sox owner Bill Veeck to rescue the team with its next pennant in 1959. Veeck revived the franchise with his "Go-Go Sox" and turned Comiskey Park into a carnival with an exploding center-field scoreboard that ignited for every Chicago homer. The party continued after Veeck sold the club—picnic tables were set up behind the fences and showers for sweaty center-field bleacher bums were added.

But by the late 1980s, after eight decades of baseball witnessed by more than 72 million fans, the "Baseball Palace of the World" was showing her age. In an ending as sentimental as its beginning, Chicago bid adieu to the original Comiskey Park in 1990. "Nothing is forever," said Chuck Comiskey, Commy's grandson. "The ballpark has served us well. It deserves a rest."

BILL VEECK'S PLAYGROUND

STEP RIGHT UP, hurry, hurry, and see baseball's greatest sideshow—the one, the only, Bill Veeck. He's the marketing whiz who brought ivy to Wrigley Field, a midget to St. Louis, Satchel Paige to Cleveland, and a lot of wackiness to Comiskey Park.

Veeck had owned clubs in Milwaukee, Cleveland, and St. Louis, giving away animals, nylons—*anything* to draw fans to his ailing franchises. In 1959, Veeck brought his show to Chicago for a two-act performance with the White Sox. His grandest achievement at Comiskey was installing its exploding scoreboard, which erupted after every Sox home run. The franchise's fortunes soared, but a year later, an ailing Veeck retired. He returned for an encore in 1976 and later presented his

most appalling promotion: Disco Demolition Night (actually his son's idea) brought a sellout crowd on July 12, 1979, but the Sox forfeited the second game of a doubleheader with Detroit after fires ignited and rowdy fans stormed the field. Veeck's pleas for order were ignored. Scorned by the baseball elite, Bill Veeck sold the team two years later.

THE TIGERS' LAIR: TIGER STADIUM

Top: One of the most famous intersections in 20th-century American sports, the corner of Michigan and Trumbull avenues was a popular summertime destination for Detroiters and fans of baseball. *Above:* This 1970s pennant displays the pride that Tigers fans had in their ballpark. Detroit won six American League pennants during their stay at Tiger Stadium (from 1912 to 1999), and followed four of them with World Series victories.

Sure, we all know there's no crying in baseball. But no one ever panned the notion of a good old-fashioned hug. And, certainly, no one could blame Detroit baseball fans for expressing their affection for Tiger Stadium.

It's said that the ballpark that anchored "The Corner" for more than eight decades is the only stadium ever hugged by its fans. On two occasions, with wrecking balls poised to swing, hundreds of forlorn yet determined Tiger Stadium Fan Club members circled the

ballpark and locked hands to offer a collective hug. No stadium before or since has been so embraced.

Baseball had been played in Detroit's Corktown neighborhood at the corner of Michigan and Trumbull avenues since Grover Cleveland was president and Henry Ford came up with a better idea. While the city around it redefined itself, enduring triumphs and tragedies, Tiger Stadium was an anchor. In its life span, that corner was home to the most enduring address in all of sports.

Baseballs were first hit at "The Corner" in 1896 inside wooden Bennett Park, which was originally home to the city's National League team, the Wolverines. It took its name in honor of Charlie Bennett, a former Detroit ballplayer who lost his legs in a train accident. Built on the site of a former hay market, Bennett Park was, by most accounts, diminutive and dingy, and when the late-afternoon sun appeared, it shined directly into batters' eyes. Its infield was also hazardous, with cobblestone left from the market protruding from under a thin layer of dirt. It was here in 1905 that feisty and formidible Ty Cobb first displayed his uncanny hitting tools, elevating the Tigers toward the top of the American League. As the team reeled off three straight pennants at decade's end, Tigers owner Frank J. Navin, wary of expanding his dilapidated park, decided that he had no choice but to start fresh.

Navin Field opened in 1912, but the opening of Boston's Fenway Park, which hosted its inaugural game that same day, overshadowed the occasion. Bennett caught the ceremonial first pitch, and Cobb, as usual, stole the show, swiping home in a 6–5 win over Cleveland before a thunderous standing-room-only crowd. Detroit finally had a ballpark that fit its winning club. Navin's ballpark provided seating for more than 23,000 inside a sturdy steel-and-concrete single-deck grandstand that spanned the foul lines. An isolated set of bleachers was perched in right field. Home plate was shifted away from Trumbull Avenue. To fit its urban landscape, the original outfield

was 467 feet deep to center field, 345 to left, and 370 to right; alterations in later years shortened these distances. A second deck was added 11 seasons later, as was a press box, which was so close to the field that reporters were sometimes in peril.

For a time, canvas hung atop the outfield bleachers to block the views of "wildcat watchers" on neighboring rooftops. In the 1910s, Detroit saw an infusion of blue-collar workers; its population more than doubled to a million as it took its place as the center of the automobile world.

Navin and his Tigers persisted through the Cobb era's end before finally winning a World Series in 1935 behind the exploits of sluggers Charlie Gehringer and Hank Greenberg. Navin suffered a heart attack and died that same fall. Investor Walter Briggs took

Below: This postcard from early in the 20th century shows that Navin Field had many obstructed-view seats, but that didn't stop fans from coming out to support greats like Ty Cobb and Harry Heilmann. *Bottom:* Navin Field, Briggs Stadium, and Tiger Stadium were all monikers worn by a ballpark that stood as an iconic major-league setting for most of the 20th century.

SWEET FAREWELL

They gathered at "The Corner" for one final hug. The fight to spare Tiger Stadium was long over. "Today, there is crying in baseball. Goodbye old friend," read a homemade banner.

The final game at Tiger Stadium, which was played on September 27, 1999, brought a swell of emotions from longtime fans and old-time Tigers. When Royals outfielder Carlos Beltran swung and missed Tiger hurler Todd Jones's 2–2 pitch in the top of the ninth, the game was truly over. Never was a Tiger win so bittersweet. Greats such as Al Kaline, Alan Trammell, and Lou Whitaker took the field with dozens of other players, past and present, for a final bow. Relatives of former owners and 19th-century Detroit catcher Charlie Bennett, whose name was affixed to the Tigers' first ballpark, were on hand.

Elden Auker, a Tigers pitcher from the 1930s, hurled a final pitch, and legendary team broadcaster Ernie Harwell offered a eulogy of sorts before home plate was escorted to the Tigers' new lair. Ten years later, a wrecking ball took a final swing at Tiger Stadium.

Left: Flamethrowing Bob Gibson and the St. Louis Cardinals won Game 4 of the 1968 World Series at Tiger Stadium, but Detroit rebounded for a seven-game Series victory. *Below:* This is the program for the 1941 All-Star Game. During the contest, one of the great moments in baseball history took place when Ted Williams launched a three-run walk-off homer to give the AL a 7–5 win.

the helm and remodeled Navin Field during the 1937–38 off-season. To spur more home runs, Briggs shrank the park's outfield, enclosing it for good and creating the park's trademark ten-foot upper-deck overhang and baseball's only double-deck bleachers. Greenberg immediately benefited, hitting a record 39 dingers in his home park in 1938 (he had 58 total). Briggs reaped benefits as well, offering seating to 53,000 while maintaining the park's intimacy. "I could hear everything that was said," recalled third baseman George Kell.

Aside from routine maintenance, Briggs Stadium (as it was rechristened after the overhaul) remained unchanged over the next several decades. History, however, continued to unfurl. In the decisive game of the 1934 World Series, St. Louis left fielder Joe "Ducky" Medwick, after tussling with Detroit's

Marv Owen, was showered with debris tossed by angry Tiger fans. To restore order, Commissioner Kenesaw Landis's only option was to remove Medwick. It didn't help the Tigers, who lost the game and the Series. Five summers later, Yankee great Lou Gehrig's consecutive game streak came to a sad end within the stadium's confines. Shortly thereafter, two more AL pennants came Detroit's way (in 1940 and '45), and in 1945, the Tigers won their second World

9th ANNUAL ALL-STAR GAME *Official* SOUVENIR *Program* 25¢
AMERICAN LEAGUE vs NATIONAL LEAGUE
JULY 8th 1941 – AT DETROIT

Briggs Stadium
HOME OF THE AMERICAN LEAGUE CHAMPIONS

Series, blasting the Chicago Cubs in Game 7, 9–3.

The park was the last in the American League to begin hosting night games, preferring natural sunlight to artificial glare until 1948. In 1961, new ownership renamed the park "Tiger Stadium." That decade brought urban unrest and decay, conditions that were slightly soothed by a World Series title in 1968. That year, Tigers players, like outfielder Willie Horton, personally ventured into the streets to help ease tensions. Talks of building a new park began at around this time. Traditionalists banded together, however, and new owner John Fetzer lost his bid for a new park when voters rejected his financing plans.

Two years later, plans for a domed suburban stadium to house Fetzer's club fell through. Instead, following a fire in 1977, there were considerable renovations made to The Corner. Blue and orange plastic seats replaced wood, blue paint splashed the grandstands, and a state-of-the-art outfield scoreboard was erected. Outside, off-white and blue siding adorned the park. Unfortunately, the fight to save Tiger Stadium was only festering. A battle that divided the populace pitted those who wanted to renovate the park for its history and significance against those who sought to reinvigorate the struggling city and its downtown with a brand new facility.

"Should we tear down the White House or the Statue of Liberty just because they are old?" *Green Cathedrals* author Philip Lowry asked.

The Tiger Stadium Fan Club—whose members joined hands to hug the park in 1988 and again two years later— enlisted state and local leaders to aid their cause. Tigers owner Mike Ilitch eventually won out, securing enough public financing to break ground on a new downtown stadium in 1997. Crying in baseball was allowed just once in Detroit; for many, it happened when Tiger Stadium hosted its final ballgame on September 27, 1999.

Right: Fans flooded the Tiger Stadium field and celebrated in the streets of the Greater Detroit area after the Tigers beat the Padres for the 1984 World Series title. *Below:* This 1999 game between Detroit and St. Louis was one of the last at Tiger Stadium. The park closed at the end of that season and was demolished ten years later.

FOREVER FENWAY

Peter Mark Roget would have easily exhausted his thesaurus after just an inning at Fenway Park. And he's not alone; many a wordsmith has walked out of the shrine waxing prose that left few superlatives standing.

There's Fenway's seemingly appropriate spot in Back Bay, which is among Boston's most hallowed academic and artistic neighborhoods. Inside the park's stately brick exterior facade, there's green—real green, baseball green, Monster green. Above that monumental wall sits a flapping net that's seen jittering as it snatches baseballs in countless grainy replays of magical and heartbreaking Fenway moments. There's baseball's simplest scoreboard hung on that legendary wall, shooting eyes toward the oddest outfield contours ever conceived, all the way to the "Right Field Belly." Foul territory? There's nary room for two fielders to stand side by side. And finally, for baseball fans, there isn't a bad seat from which to inhale it all.

"Baseball appeals because of its close analogy to life, and Boston's pea-green bandbox captures the bizarre tragicomedy of the summer game better than any other setting," baseball historian Michael Benson wrote in his book, *Ballparks of North America*.

As Fenway Park passed its 100th birthday, its legend only became further etched in lore. Like a lifelong friend, Fenway is seemingly always there.

Fenway—so named because of its location in a Boston marsh called "The Fens"—opened on April 20, 1912; it was

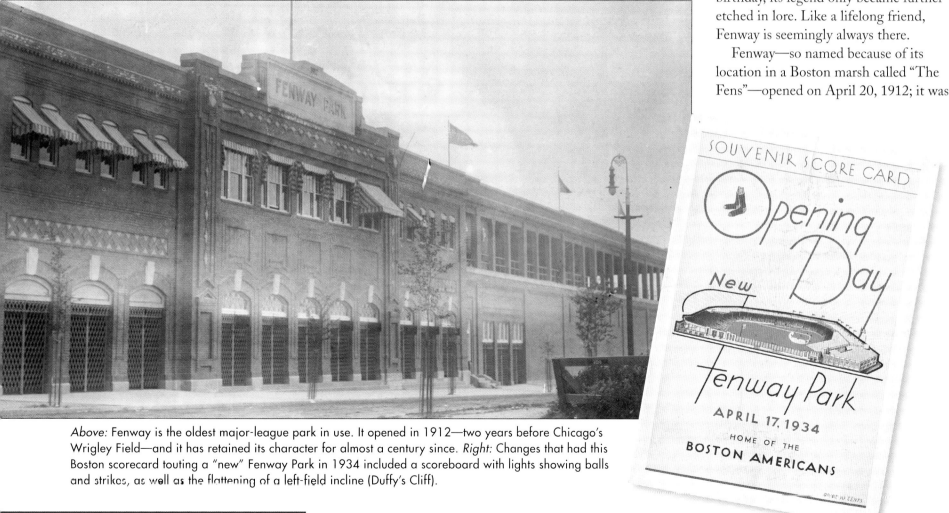

Above: Fenway is the oldest major-league park in use. It opened in 1912—two years before Chicago's Wrigley Field—and it has retained its character for almost a century since. *Right:* Changes that had this Boston scorecard touting a "new" Fenway Park in 1934 included a scoreboard with lights showing balls and strikes, as well as the flattening of a left-field incline (Duffy's Cliff).

SOUVENIR SCORE CARD

Opening Day

New

Fenway Park

APRIL 17, 1934

HOME OF THE
BOSTON AMERICANS

yet another jewel in baseball's classic ballpark era. That day, the Sox defeated the New York Highlanders in 11 innings, 7–6. The park originally featured a deeply set single-deck grandstand and bleachers that accommodated 27,000 patrons. Its reception among critics paled in comparison to those received by the more ornate contemporary parks in Philadelphia and Pittsburgh. But Fenway Park proved to agree with the Crimson Hose lineup, as the Red Sox went on to win 105 games that first season on the way to the franchise's second World Series victory. Three more championships would follow in the next six summers at Fenway.

The Red Sox were led by center fielder Tris Speaker, who quickly mastered the quirky walls behind him, the deepest of which stood approximately 550 feet from the plate. (This far-flung pasture would later be known as "The Triangle.") Flanking Speaker were Duffy Lewis and Harry Hooper, the other members of Boston's much-heralded "Million-Dollar Outfield." Lewis was charged with mastering the ten-foot rise toward the left-field fence, which was subsequently called "Duffy's Cliff." On the mound, the Crimson Hose featured a powerful southpaw named George Herman Ruth—an undisciplined-but-athletic, beer-swigging, hot-dog-munching specimen who teammates simply called "Babe."

Despite the fact that the Sox won yet another title in 1918, attendance at Fenway slumped, and owner Harry Frazee responded by holding a sale of his best talent—most shockingly Ruth—sending the franchise into a decades-long tailspin that's often called the "Curse of the Bambino." Frustrated fans avoided Fenway through the 1920s, and serious talks about the Red Sox vacating the ballpark to become tenants of their National League neighbors at the much larger Braves Field were held. For a spell, Red Sox games on Sundays, which were not allowed by law to be played at Fenway, were held at the Braves' venue.

For many Red Sox fans, the franchise's most pivotal date is February 21, 1933—the day Tom Yawkey turned 30 years old and inherited $7 million dollars from his parents' estate. Baseball was already in the family bloodline—Yawkey's uncle and adopted parent, Bill Yawkey, was a co-owner of the Detroit Tigers. It was

Above: Players, spectators, and a marching band stand at attention for a 1924 Fenway Park flag-raising. It came during a run of 15 consecutive losing seasons for the Red Sox. *Left:* Ads adorned the walls and the flagpole was in fair territory, but the Fenway Park that hosted this 1917 game is quite similar to the one that the Red Sox call home today.

through this connection that Tom had developed a friendship with his uncle's star player, Ty Cobb, who urged Yawkey to use his wealth to buy the Sox. Four days later, Yawkey was in the owner's

Left: Fenway Park is known for the "Green Monster," as this pin indicates. The towering left-field wall is a celebrated feature of the ballpark. *Below:* Though stadiums elsewhere offer more modern amenities and hold several thousand more onlookers, a sunny summer day at Fenway Park is tough for a baseball fan to beat.

seat, a spot he'd occupy for 44 years—a tenure unmatched by any other owner. With Yawkey in charge, change was afoot. Sox fans took notice, more than doubling the attendance at Fenway Park from Yawkey's first season to his second. "Yawkey is the last of the dilettante sportsmen, the gentlemen owners, the George Apleys of baseball," Melvin Maddocks would write later in *Sports Illustrated*. "Where would Fenway be without him?"

After two significant fires, Fenway underwent a major reconstruction in 1934 that saw it become close to what fans visit today. Gone was Duffy's Cliff.

Up, up, and up went a massive 37-foot wall, which was initially constructed of tin and supported by railroad ties. Its distance from home plate has always been questioned and various measurements have never agreed. More apparent were the unpredictable bounces that confounded many left fielders, as balls ricocheted off the wall's colorful ads that promoted Gem razor blades and Lifebuoy soap.

Advertising disappeared under green paint 13 seasons later, and a Monster was born. A screen measuring more than 23 feet high was mounted above the wall in 1936, a move that was needed to keep

home runs from crashing through windows along Lansdowne Street. To retrieve balls snared in the net, a ladder was affixed 13 feet above the playing field; balls that struck it remained in play. The Green Monster remains the unpredictable signature trademark of Fenway and perhaps all of baseball. It has made the sport into a game of chance in Boston by swiping hits from batters, playing surefire doubles into frustrating singles, and enabling bloopers to float over as home runs.

Despite Yawkey's best efforts, the Red Sox could not shake the Curse of the Bambino, though three pennant-winning teams—1946, 1967, and 1975—played in but lost World Series while Yawkey was alive. And the 1986 near-miss seemed to shake the BoSox faithful to their core. It was not until 2004 that the Red Sox were able to exorcise some demons by staging a near-impossible comeback, winning four straight games after being down three games to none to the rival Yankees to win the ALCS. They went on to finish the deal by sweeping the St. Louis Cardinals in the World Series. The Red Sox have since returned to the World Series in 2007 and 2013, winning both times.

FENWAY GETS A FACELIFT

WHEN HE BOUGHT the Red Sox, Tom Yawkey was young, with millions to invest in his team and their home, Fenway Park. Much work was needed.

Yawkey went to work on Fenway in the winter of 1933–34. He had permanent concrete bleachers installed along the third-base line, where wooden bleachers had been razed in 1926 as the result of a fire. Fenway's second fire, which was in January 1934, didn't dampen his enthusiasm.

Working with haste to complete his renovations by Opening Day, Yawkey oversaw the addition of 10,000 more seats, which raised the park's capacity to 37,500. Wood stands gave way to concrete and steel. A four-foot fence was installed around the grandstand roof to snare foul balls. A slope at the left-field fence was effectively removed and replaced by a 37-foot wall—the future "Green Monster." All around the outfield, the fences were moved in; in center, the depths were reduced from 488 feet to 420. Yawkey's changes, which transformed Fenway into approximately what we see today, helped double attendance in 1934.

"DEM BUMS" FIND A HOME IN EBBETS FIELD

Ebbets Field became something of a shrine for thousands of Dodgers fans. The park grew along with the club's popularity, its capacity surging from 18,000 to more than 32,000.

Ebbets Field. Even outside of Brooklyn, these two words evoke thoughts of baseball romanticism and simple quaintness.

Through books, movies, and effusive newspaper articles, the park and the scrappy Brooklyn Dodgers came to symbolize Americans who saw themselves as overachieving underdogs. The Dodgers, "Dem Bums," belonged to Brooklyn—and Ebbets Field was their Flatbush sanctuary. The ballpark was opened in 1913 by Dodger owner Charles Ebbets on a four-acre parcel amid shanties and atop a garbage dump that had been used by residents to graze their pigs. Ebbets went broke buying up the land, but still managed to deliver a classic park.

As they walk through the rotunda—the formidable, arch-windowed main entrance of Ebbets Field—fans realized that the game held significance. Under their shoes lay an exquisite Italian marble floor highlighted with a stitched baseball design. Twenty-seven feet above hovered a stucco ceiling. Its focal point was an ornate chandelier, which cast 12 arms that were shaped like baseball bats and held just as many light globes.

Further inside awaited an enclosed green pasture on which legends—Robinson, Snider, Lavagetto, Campanella—frolicked. Fans were so close—the batter's box was just 64 feet from the backstop—that they could hear the catcher's chatter and see the expressions on the players' faces. The bullpens were placed inside the sparse distance between the stands and foul lines. The right-field fence was a measly 301 feet away from home plate thanks to Bedford Avenue, which ran beyond it. Left field proved much more daunting at 419 feet, and the center-field fence was an almost unreachable 450 feet. Ebbets Field also had its quirky side—the wall from right-center sloped outward, and an adjacent 19-foot wall plastered with ads was capped with an equally high screen. Fielding shots off these walls amounted to an art form.

Originally, a double-deck grandstand that held 18,000 cradled the infield, but as the team's popularity soared, so did the stadium's seating capacity. And with its expanding grandstands that eventually engulfed most of the park, Ebbets Field transformed a pitcher's dream into a hurler's nightmare. Its famous scoreboard—which sported a Schaefer Beer sign whose "h" or "e" letters would light up when a ruling was issued for a hit or error—arrived in 1930.

Ebbets struck gold in this section of Brooklyn, which was once called

Pigtown. Before long, fans from all over the city could use the subway or a trolley to get to the park, opening up vast markets of possible customers for Ebbets. Dodging those trolleys became so commonplace for Brooklyn fans that the team—which had been called the Bridegrooms, Superbas, and Robins—eventually settled on the "Dodgers" name in 1932.

The Dodgers had a natural rivalry with the New York Giants. Under the firm hand of manager John McGraw, the Giants fashioned a dynasty while Dodgers fans developed chips on their shoulders. But outside of pennant-winning seasons in 1916 and 1920, the Dodgers consistently sat in the NL's second division. Despite this, if you lived in Brooklyn, you rooted for the Dodgers.

This allegiance bore fruit during a span from 1941 to 1956, when the Dodgers appeared in seven World Series, all against the high-and-mighty New York Yankees. Not only were those Dodgers famous, Brooklyn *fans* gained their own fifteen minutes of fame. "Howling" Hilda Chester clanged her obnoxious cowbell in the upper-deck bleachers, and the self-deprecating Dodger Sym-Phony band would attempt to spark rallies.

The beauty of the park, the blue caps and lettering over white jerseys, and the uncompromising bond between the players and fans made the franchise's move to Los Angeles after the 1957 season that much more stunning. The stadium's funeral wouldn't occur until 1960, when a wrecking ball took its final swipe at Ebbets. Memories are all that remain. "Ebbets Field," historian Michael Benson noted, "was maybe the best ballpark ever, home of the greatest pain and greatest joy and home of the biggest family."

Ten times between 1939 and 1952, the Dodger-blue turnstiles of Ebbets Field were twirled by paying fans more often than those at any other National League park.

Top left: June 15, 1938, saw history made at Ebbets Field. The Reds' Johnny Vander Meer pitched his second consecutive no-hitter, blanking the Dodgers in the first night game played outside Cincinnati. *Bottom left:* The Brooklyn neighborhood that housed Ebbets was commonly known as Flatbush, though some called it "Pigtown" before the ballpark's presence changed its course.

CROSLEY FIELD SUITS THE REDS

Below: These red seats from Crosley Field sported the logo of the Reds. Crosley hosted more than one million fans for the first time in 1956, a milestone it repeated the following year and twice during the 1960s. *Right:* The first night game in major-league history took place at Crosley on May 24, 1935. President Franklin Roosevelt lit the stadium before the Reds edged the Phillies, 2–1.

For 86 years, summer was signaled in Cincinnati by the thwack of bats at Findlay Street and Western Avenue. For the majority of those years, it was Crosley Field that beckoned.

The park opened in 1912 as Redland Field, and it served as home to the Cincinnati Reds into the 1970 season. In between, Crosley provided its customers an experience all its own. Perhaps the most notable of Crosley's nuances was its four-foot incline near the left-field fence. Called the "terrace," this incline sometimes caused players to bumble their ways through games. Babe Ruth, well past his prime and winding down his career with the Boston Braves, once stumbled while chasing down a fly ball, brushed his aging legs off, and promptly exited Crosley in disgust. But the terrace remained.

Crosley—which was renamed in 1934 for its radio- and car-building owner Powel Crosley Jr.—was neither ornate nor decorative. As a park, it was simple. Its 20,000 seating capacity was considered modest for its day. It featured a double-deck grandstand around the infield with a single-deck pavilion to the outfield along each foul line. An isolated bleacher section sat beyond the right-field fence in the shadow of paper-company warehouses. Along left field were the player clubhouses, which offered a personal touch for the park—players, on good days and bad, had to walk past crowds of fans on their way to and from the locker rooms. Once inside, players could relax with a game of pool in a separate lounge.

Adding to its individuality was an in-play scoreboard in left-center field that rose 58 feet from the ground. Beyond the left-field wall was the Superior Towel & Linen Service building, a prominent fixture of York Street. It carried a sign for the Siebler Suit company that offered players new duds if they managed to strike it. Reds outfielder Wally Post boasted that he won 16 suits; Giants star Willie Mays managed to score seven suits during his visits.

Under Crosley's ownership and General Manager Larry MacPhail's leadership, the Reds excelled. More seats were eventually added, and the spacious outfield from the dead-ball era was reduced to encourage home runs. On May 24, 1935, to increase attendance

After Crosley's fences were brought in, operators of its one-of-a-kind scoreboard grew busy. The Reds got three homers and ten RBI from Walker Cooper during this 23–4 win in 1949.

during the Great Depression, President Franklin D. Roosevelt threw a switch in Washington and illuminated Crosley Field for baseball's first night game. Crosley served the Reds well as the team won back-to-back pennants in 1939 and 1940. Crosley also became the first major-league facility to provide a home to a Negro League team when the Cuban Stars of the 1920s started playing there.

As baseball's modern era took hold in the 1960s, it became clear that Crosley's days were numbered. The stadium was shuttered after a 5–4 Reds win over the Giants on June 28, 1970, before a near-capacity crowd. Although it was demolished two years later, Crosley Field lives on in Blue Ash, Ohio, where a life-size replica of the old ballpark's scoreboard, walls, and playing dimensions, stands.

PALACE OF THE FANS

At any moment, or so it seemed, some Greek god dressed in a toga might dig into the batter's box at the Palace of the Fans. But this was early 20th-century Cincinnati, not ancient Athens.

Reds' owner John Brush intended to build a palace to replace the burned-down League Park. When the stadium opened in 1902, was the most luxurious ballpark that anyone had ever seen.

The focal point inside the park was an imposing triangular pediment—supported by hand-carved Corinthian columns that rose above the infield backstop—with "Cincinnati" chiseled in stone. Around the infield were opera-like semicircular "Fashion Boxes" that sat the Queen City's discerning elite. Along the first-base and third-base lines, at level with the field, ran "Rooter's Row," where fans were served by waiters who offered beer—12 glasses for a dollar. The *Chicago Tribune* effusively called Brush's palace "the finest plant in the league . . . furnished in every detail." Every detail, that is, except players' dugouts and clubhouses. Damaged by neglect and a fire in the grandstand, the Palace closed in 1911.

This is a silver ticket to the 1902 dedication of the Palace of the Fans.

BRAVES FIELD SETS THE STANDARD FOR SIZE

The business of baseball was flourishing, with new parks rising up around both leagues, but July 4, 1914, saw owner James Gaffney's Boston Braves in a pretty typical position: They were dead last in the National League, 15 games behind the Giants.

The hastily constructed third version of the South End Grounds—the spartan home of the Braves for 20 years—was lifeless. But then the baseball gods went to work. By September 2, 1914, the Braves had surged into first place. By October, they were the "Miracle Braves"

and World Series champions. By the following summer, Gaffney was opening his new ballpark.

Braves Field was bigger and grander than any of the ten other ballparks that had risen around baseball the previous five seasons. With a million-dollar sticker price and room for 40,000, it was dubbed the sport's first "super stadium." Its playing field was equally imposing—its shallowest fence was 402 feet away from home. Clearly, Gaffney favored speed and pitching—it took ten seasons before a hitter (Frank Snyder) cleared the

left-field fence. During that time, there were more than 200 inside-the-park home runs hit within its confines.

Gaffney had been eyeing a new ballpark since 1912, when he purchased 13 acres of the Allston Golf Club on Commonwealth Avenue, just off the Charles River and a mile from Fenway Park. Legend has it that a dozen horses and mules died during a cave-in while the park was under construction and were left along the third-base line, buried under grass that was brought over from South End Grounds.

Nonetheless, Braves Field swelled past capacity when the park opened on August 18, 1915. With an estimated 42,000 fans on hand (some of whom

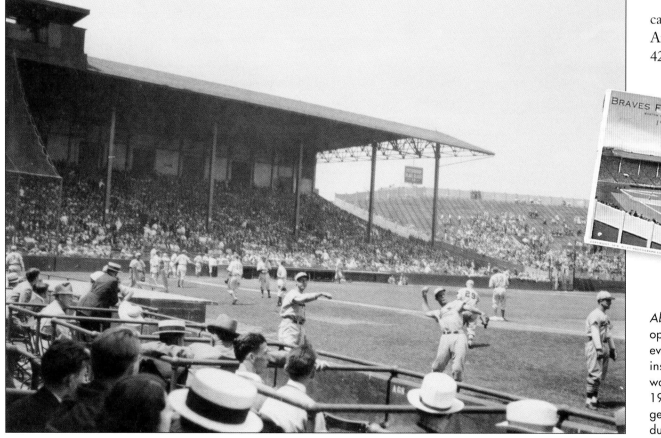

Above: As this postcard shows, Braves Field opened in 1915 with a big price tag and an even bigger outfield, which led to exciting inside-the-park home runs. *Left:* Braves Field was known as the "Bee Hive" when this 1938 game took place. The Bees were generally harmless to National League foes during their run from 1936 to '40.

took a trolley that stopped just inside the park), it was hailed as the largest gathering ever to watch a baseball game. The park provided four seating sections: an 18,000-capacity, single-deck roofed grandstand around the infield; uncovered pavilions in left and right that each held 10,000; and a noteworthy set of bleachers called the "Jury Box" in right-center that held 2,000 people, each of whom plunked down two bits a ticket.

Miracles failed to repeat for the Braves, and after the stadium's grand opening, the team slipped back into the second division, a slump that would last for decades. As attendance dwindled, so too did the outfields at Braves Field, as the club tried to join in baseball's home run infatuation of the 1920s. Alas, for a spell of 30 seasons—from 1917 to 1946—the Braves never finished higher than fourth place. A nickname change in the late 1930s to the Bees—the park was called the "Bee Hive"—didn't sting opponents. Despite a brief revival in 1948, when the Braves captured the pennant, the team didn't draw well so it packed up and moved to Milwaukee in 1953. Braves Field endures to this day as part of the Boston University campus.

TEN YEARS AFTER

IN 1915, TY Cobb squinted at the distant fences of new Braves Field and predicted no one could clear them. And in fact, no one hit one out to left field until Giants catcher Frank "Pancho" Snyder muscled one out in 1925—*ten years later!*

Braves owner James Gaffney loved the thrill of an inside-the-park home run, and there would be no 300-foot cheapies flying over fences in his new stadium. Its seating was super-size and so was its playing field—402 feet down each line and a Ruthian 550 feet to dead center. Adding to hitters' frustrations was a prevailing wind that blew in from the Charles River. Gaffney got his wish: In the park's first 12 years, only seven balls passed over the fence. During the same period, 209 homers stayed in play.

In the 1920s, however, the home run came into vogue. Gaffney's dead-ball delight had passed. For the 1928 season, the fences at Braves Field were dramatically drawn in, sending hitters into a home-run frenzy. Problem was, opposing teams were hitting most of the homers off Braves pitching. Afterward, the fences' distances seemed to fluctuate with the Charles River breeze.

WRIGLEY FIELD: WALLS OF IVY

We have at least three baseball traditions for which to thank "Lucky Charlie" Weeghman: souvenir foul balls, concession stands, and those four acres of bluegrass-laden friendly confines of Wrigley Field.

Weeghman didn't yet own the Chicago Cubs when he built the ballpark at Clark and Addison on the city's yet-to-be-developed North Side. He named the stadium after himself, and Weeghman Park opened in 1914 to host his Chicago Chi-Feds, an entry in the fledgling Federal League (which sought to challenge the American and National leagues). The park was originally a single-deck affair that sat 14,000 fans, cost $250,000, and featured a beautiful pasture of lush Merion bluegrass. While the Chi-Feds (becoming the Whales for the 1915 season) thrived, at times outdrawing Chicago's Cubs and White Sox, the league didn't—it died after two seasons, taking "Lucky Charlie's" team with it. But Weeghman's ballpark has endured as Wrigley Field, an American treasure for more than a century.

Above: The Yankees won the 1938 Series. The Cubs also lost the 1945 Series to Detroit before ending a 108-year championship drought by bringing the 2016 title to the Wrigley Field faithful.

Once a $10-a-week waiter in the 1890s, Weeghman spun a chain of lunch counters into an $8-million empire while earning the "Lucky" nickname. After his failed venture with the Whales, Weeghman purchased the Cubs and relocated the franchise from the ancient West Side Park for the 1916 season.

Weeghman strove to make baseball fan-friendly. Joa, an honest-to-goodness live bear cub, was housed in a cage outside the park on Addison Street. Fans could keep foul balls that they caught at Weeghman, a major no-no at other parks. Complaints of vendors blocking views of the action prompted him to add concession stands, another baseball first. Weeghman's dance with lady luck ended in 1918, the same year the Cubs won the pennant in a season shortened by World War I. Struck by financial disaster, he sold the club to William Wrigley Jr., heir to the Wrigley chewing-gum fortune. Wrigley saw to a seating expansion of the park—he cut the grandstand, put half on rollers to move it, and filled the gap with more grandstands. He moved

the entire playing field to the southwest, added an upper deck, and finally, in 1926, changed the park's name to "Wrigley Field." With seating for 40,000, Chicago fans turned out at the unheard-of rate of a million or more a season by the late 1920s to see the powerful likes of Hack Wilson, Riggs Stephenson, and Rogers Hornsby, who managed 39 homers in 1929 while winding down his Hall of Fame career at Wrigley.

Cub fans had World Series games to attend in 1929 and witnessed the historic 1932 Fall Classic, in which Babe Ruth is said to have pointed to the center-field bleachers, promising to smack a homer off Cubs pitcher Charlie Root. The Bambino delivered. "I'd play for half my salary if I could hit in this dump all the time," Ruth boasted to reporters.

P. K. Wrigley took over for his father in 1932 and went about promoting his park as well as his baseball team, making a visit as unpredictable as the Lake Michigan winds, which can change a game at any moment. The young Wrigley had some help from an up-and-coming baseball executive named Bill Veeck Jr. Wrigley Field's fabled bleachers came to life in 1937, along with the Boston ivy that still covers its brick outfield walls. Veeck's idea for the ivy was inspired by a unique design at Bush Stadium in Indianapolis. (Veeck also planted eight Chinese elms and Japanese bittersweet plants, but none survived.) A bright-green manually operated scoreboard, which still posts numbers today, also made its first appearance that year, towering 85 feet above the field and atop the center-field bleachers. At the time, Wrigley fans were the only to track the scores of games from other cities. In 1941, organ music sounded Cub rallies for the first time.

P. K. Wrigley was intent on keeping his park a suitable and comfortable place for ladies and children. Even the playing

Above: The famed ivy on Wrigley Field's walls was planted in 1937. It was part of Bill Veeck Jr.'s beautification project for the new outfield bleachers. *Left:* A moving ramp seemed state-of-the-art in 1956, but Wrigley Field now stands as the second-oldest stadium in use in the major leagues. Only Boston's Fenway Park is older.

BALLPARK PICASSO

THEY ALL KNEW Otis Shepard; maybe not his face, but certainly the faces he drew for the Wrigley family. His unique works of art were prominently displayed on souvenir programs at Wrigley Field for better than three decades.

Shepard came to the Wrigley Company in 1932 as Philip K. Wrigley's choice to be the company's art director. His assignments included Cubs scorecard covers, as well as uniform designs and advertising campaigns for the company's chewing gum franchises. By the time he left the company in 1962, he was considered one of America's finest poster designers. Shepard's airbrush artwork on the club's ten-cent scorecards was unquestionably his own—simplistic yet colorful, whether the subject was bold, square-jaw ballplayers or a fuzzy bear cub in a straw hat.

The sliding bear cub on this cover, from 1941, is typical of the work of Otis Shepard.

In art circles, Shepard is credited with perfecting a distinctive, modern airbrush technique for Wrigley's fresh-face Doublemint Gum campaign in the 1930s. Shepard's work also included uniform designs, some of which were ridiculed at the time of their proposal but later copied (including zippered jerseys, powder-blue "away" jerseys, and vests).

field was immaculate, thanks in large part to groundskeeper Bobby Dorr (who, in the 1930s, lived in a six-room apartment that was located at Wrigley Field's left field corner gate).

One amenity that didn't come to Wrigley Field at the time was lights. While most parks added illumination after the Reds hosted the first night game in 1935, all Cubs home games for decades thereafter were afternoon tilts. It wasn't until 1988 that Cubs brass and their tradition-minded fan base relented and allowed lights to be installed.

In the meantime, the Cubs kept winning. Pennants came in 1935, '38, and '45, but something was missing: a World Series championship, something that had eluded the Cubs since 1908. The dry spell would become more legendary with each passing summer, decade after painful decade. Wrigley Field, however, would

only grow in stature and prestige. The slogan "Friendly Confines" was made famous by Cubs great Ernie Banks, a Hall of Fame shortstop and first baseman who played 19 seasons at Wrigley—but never on a pennant-winner.

By the 1960s, losing was almost expected, and a group of ten "Bleacher Bums" made their first appearance in 1966. They quickly grew into thousands. Although Chicago's rowdier side had revealed itself in the bleachers for decades, this collection of die-hards made its mark with acrimony, vigor, and humor. So popular were their actions, a play and two TV movies titled *Bleacher Bums* documented their party. It wasn't long before Wrigley bleacher-dwellers began the tradition of throwing opponents' home runs back onto the field. Fans who didn't buy tickets found free peeks from rooftops along Waveland and Sheffield

High winds, a manually operated scoreboard, and team flags depicting the order of the National League standings are signature elements of an afternoon at Wrigley Field.

avenues, a tradition that has continued unabated since the park opened.

Fans embraced their celebrated status as "Loveable Losers," reveled in "Take Me Out to the Ballgame" renditions and traded Harry Caray impersonations for years, but were long overdue for a celebration by 2016. After reaching the playoffs in '15 under the brilliant eye of front-office whiz Theo Epstein, the 2016 Cubbies took baseball by storm. Emerging victorious in one of the most epic World Series Game 7s in history, generations of Cubs fans hardly knew what to do when their 108-year drought ended in a championship. Some five million spectators—one of the largest gatherings of humanity in world history—attended the parade. Renovations to Wrigley and the "Wrigleyville" neighborhood around it have changed the landscape to some

extent. But the Wrigley Field experience retains the feeling of walking into a Rockwell drawing, back to simple worries and American dreams—all in the shadow of a 2016 championship banner.

Top: "Bleacher Bums" and rooftop views have contributed to the romance of Cub fandom, and are among the many reasons Wrigley has become known as the "Friendly Confines." *Middle:* Tradition took a backseat to progress (although some would argue that description) in 1988, when Wrigley Field became the last major-league stadium to install lights for night baseball. This pennant shows the light standards in place. *Right:* It has changed from time to time, just as the faces of the Cubs have, but this iconic marquee has greeted North Side fans outside Wrigley Field since the 1930s.

YANKEE STADIUM: THE HOUSE THAT RUTH BUILT

The red, white, and blue bunting that marked All-Star games, World Series, and other major sporting events came to be standard garb for "The House That Ruth Built."

For nine minutes, the applause inside Yankee Stadium was deafening. It was perhaps the only time the great Mickey Mantle was silenced. Only when he began to speak, evoking the memory of another storied Yankee, was the New York crowd hushed. "I often wondered how a man who knew he was going to die could stand here and say he was the luckiest man in the world," Mantle said at his 1969 farewell. "But now, I think I know how Lou Gehrig felt."

To those who played the game and to those who watched, Yankee Stadium was far more than "The House That Ruth Built." It was the house of Joltin' Joe, Whitey, Reggie, Donnie Baseball, and Derek—all Yankee greats who require no formal introduction. It was the house of the eloquent Bob Sheppard behind the PA mic, the genial Eddie Layton on the organ, and the unmistakable Mel Allen in the broadcast booth. Somehow, the ballpark got inside the hearts of not only fans, but also players who toiled and won there over eight decades in the Bronx. Yankee Stadium was New York, and New York was Yankee Stadium.

Yankee Stadium, it is said, was built in 1923 out of jealousy and greed. For most

of the ten previous seasons, the Yankees played at the Polo Grounds, tenants of their National League rivals, the New York Giants. John McGraw—the diminutive, fiery field general of the Giants—had been the toast of the Big Apple since the turn of the century. His Giants were kings of the city; the Yankees were no threat to his dynasty. McGraw's mood grew darker after Babe Ruth became a Yankee, however. In Ruth's first Yankee season in 1920, the team's attendance doubled to 1.2 million, surpassing the number posted by the Giants. Before the start of 1921 season, the Yankees were given their eviction notice: They were done at the Polo Grounds after the '22 season. McGraw, it is said, looked to slay his upstart rival, believing that the Yankees could never muster enough land in Manhattan to threaten any more harm to his Giants.

Yankees owners Jacob Ruppert and Tillinghast L'Hommedieu Huston stuck it to McGraw. They found, for $600,000, a ten-acre plot right across the Harlem River and within eyeshot of the Polo Grounds. Their new park would be an in-your-face "super stadium." Ground was broken on May 5, 1922, while the Yankees marched toward their second consecutive pennant and a World Series rematch with the Giants. Osborn Engineering, a Cleveland firm, designed the massive stadium, which would seat 58,000 on three tiers. No stadium would be grander. White Construction Company workers finished building it in about 285 working days.

Yankee Stadium opened on April 18, 1923. More than 70,000 lucky souls made it through the turnstiles of the stately outer brick facade, which spoke "Yankee Stadium" with importance (20,000 were turned away). Inside, they saw the ornate frieze that hung majestically around the roof of the upper deck. Merion bluegrass rolled through an abundant outfield that reached 490 feet to the center-field fence. The power

alleys were nearly as daunting, so it's no surprise that the region was nicknamed "Death Valley" almost immediately.

The fences were much closer down the lines in left and right. Left field was inviting to righties at 280 feet, and right field, at 295, was, by no accident, an easy target for the Sultan of Swat. "I'd give a year of my life if I can hit a home run in this first game in this new park," Babe Ruth told reporters. In the third inning, he got his wish. Afterward, newspaperman Fred Lieb wrote his iconic account of the game, calling Yankee Stadium "the House That Ruth Built."

That fall, Yankee Stadium hosted its first World Series; the Yanks avenged two straight setbacks to the Giants by taking the title in six games. The Yankee Dynasty, the greatest in all of sports,

Above left: This flag that honors the 100-year anniversary of baseball flew over Yankee Stadium in 1939. The Yankees celebrated their fourth consecutive World Series title that season. *Above right:* The original Yankee Stadium was home to 26 New York world championships, and hosted its last game one year before the 2009 Yanks won another title.

took hold. The franchise would go on to win 36 more AL pennants and 25 more world championships at Yankee Stadium. The Bronx Bombers were America's team—loved by many, scorned by many more.

Prior to a massive renovation that started in 1973, Yankee Stadium underwent only subtle changes after its opening. Before the 1928 season, the grandstand in left field was extended past the foul pole. For the 1937 season, the triple decks were extended past the right-field foul pole. In 1932, a significant addition occurred with the installation of a monument dedicated to beloved Yankee skipper Miller Huggins, who led the team to six pennants and three World Series titles in the 1920s. Huggins died in 1929 at the age of 50; his monument, a marble tablet, was placed in deep center field. In 1941, a similar stone was erected to honor Gehrig, the legendary Yankee who played 2,130 consecutive games before illness forced him to retire. Gehrig gave his famous farewell address at Yankee Stadium on July 4, 1939, and died less than two years later at the age of 37. Ruth was memorialized with his former manager and teammate in 1949, a year after his death. Twenty years later, Joe DiMaggio and Mantle had plaques dedicated to them.

Yankee Stadium underwent a major renovation from 1974 to 1975, which put the Yankees in Shea Stadium, home of the Mets, for two seasons. When the overhaul was unveiled in 1976, fans were again in awe. Although criticized for costing taxpayers upward of $75 million and the removal of the legendary frieze around the grandstand, the renovations were generally met with approval. At least some of the frieze design was placed around the outfield bleachers. Obstructive poles were removed. In was Monument

Above: Yankee Stadium (right) was built across the Harlem River from the Polo Grounds, less than a mile away from the home of the New York Giants. *Bottom left:* This Joe DiMaggio plaque was destined for Monument Park in Yankee Stadium, but it was discovered that it is smaller than the original plaques, so a new larger one was cast. This one became a spectacular collector's item. *Top left:* Seven times during the 1940s and '50s, Yankee Stadium and Ebbets Field hosted crosstown World Series matchups between the Yankees and Brooklyn Dodgers. This program is from the 1956 Series.

Known to architects as a frieze, the distinct white facade that topped Yankee Stadium was considered the park's crowning glory and was recreated for its new incarnation.

A PARK FOR ALL SEASONS

JUST LIKE NEW York City, Yankee Stadium never slept. Whether it was for championship boxing, the NFL, college football, rock concerts, or religious gatherings, the lights at "The House That Ruth Built" rarely dimmed.

Just weeks after the ballpark opened in 1923, lightweight boxer Benny Leonard won a decision over Lou Tendler for the world title within its confines. Over the next 50-plus years, 30 championship bouts were held there, the most famous being the heavyweight battles between Joe Louis and Max Schmeling in 1936 and 1938. The boxing matches ended with Muhammad Ali's knockout of Ken Norton in 1976.

Yankee Stadium was also home to the New York football Giants for 18 seasons. Pro football's "Greatest Game Ever Played" was held at the venue on December 28, 1958, when the Baltimore Colts defeated the Giants in overtime for the NFL championship. The annual Notre Dame–Army game was played at Yankee Stadium almost every year from 1925 to 1946; it was the site of Knute Rockne's famous "win one for the Gipper" pep talk to his 1928 Fighting Irish.

Still, the most-attended events at the Stadium were pious. Three popes visited, and the 1958 Jehovah's Witness convention set the all-time attendance record with 123,000 visitors.

This ticket is for a benefit fight—Joe Louis versus Billy Conn—benefiting the Army Emergency Relief Fund at Yankee Stadium in 1942.

Park, a behind-the-fence museum that recognized the greatest of all Yankees. In were new, larger seats and a smaller playing field. Also in was another pennant, the first under controversial owner George Steinbrenner. Back-to-back championships followed in 1977 and '78, ending the team's 14-year title drought (the longest in Stadium history to that point).

Under Steinbrenner's watch and with baseball's biggest budget by far, the Yankees took full advantage of player free agency. Four World Series titles were captured in a five-year span from 1996 to 2000. These would be the last championships won at old Yankee Stadium, which closed after the 2008 season as the team relocated to the new Yankee Stadium, baseball's first billion-dollar ballpark. In typical New York fashion, former Yankee greats returned for a final farewell to the historic ball yard on September 21, 2008. Grown men cried.

"Every once in a while, you walk out there and just kind of remind yourself what this place is all about," recalled former Yankee outfielder Paul O'Neill.

SPORTSMAN'S DOES DOUBLE DUTY IN ST. LOUIS

St. Louis was atop the baseball world in the fall of 1944. The city's Cardinals and Browns, champions of their respective leagues, went head-to-head in the "Trolley Series." And since the teams shared the same stadium, Sportsman's Park was the place to be.

It wasn't pretty; there was nothing about it that was ornate, nothing that rang with importance. For a time, goats would graze the outfield, saving the venue's frugal owners the cost of mowing. For too long, seating was segregated among whites and blacks. But it had the

Cardinals, one of baseball's most successful franchises, showcasing some of the game's finest stars.

Opened in 1909, Sportsman's Park was one of several ballparks that operated near Dodier Street and Grand Avenue since the 19th century. Sportsman's, as writer Red Smith not-so-politely noted, bore "a garish, county fair sort of layout." But for 33 years, it housed the two St. Louis teams (in separate offices) while hosting more baseball games than any other park.

Landing first at the venue was the Browns, an American League entry, in

1902. At this time, Sportsman's Park was an unassuming 8,000-seat wood grandstand and a single set of bleachers near the foul pole in left. Six years later, Browns owner Robert Lee Hedges renovated his park, adding 10,000 seats by moving home plate to the southwest and employing steel and concrete to build a two-deck grandstand that wrapped around the infield. The park's existing grandstand was transformed into a pavilion that was located down the third-base line, and the bleachers spanned the outfield.

Fans file into Sportsman's Park for Game 3 of the 1926 World Series between the Cardinals and the Yankees. The Cards won the game, 4–0, and took the Series in seven.

The Cardinals, a National League stalwart, had played blocks away at Robison Field since 1893. They landed at Sportsman's Park in 1920 after cash-strapped team owner Sam Breadon sold Robison. Five years later, Sportsman's was expanded to hold 34,000, but the Browns rarely needed that many seats.

During their 52-season stay in St. Louis, the Browns were consistent losers, both in the standings and at the gate. In a hideous three-year stretch from 1937 to '39, they lost 316 games while drawing fewer than 370,000 fans total. This record of ineptitude is part of the magic of the 1944 World Series. The pennant was the first and only that the franchise won while in St. Louis. Naturally, they lost the Series.

The Cardinals were, by contrast, a model organization. The Cards won the NL pennant nine times during the years that they called Sportsman's home; six

times they were World Series champs. Thanks to General Manager Branch Rickey's acumen, the Cardinals developed some of baseball's greatest players, from Rogers Hornsby to Dizzy Dean to Stan Musial.

Even the great showman Bill Veeck—the P. T. Barnum of baseball executives—couldn't save the Browns. Veeck bought the club for a song in 1951 and tried everything to draw in fans. He installed Eddie Gaedel—all 3'7" of him—as a pinch-hitting publicity stunt during a game against Detroit. Gaedel walked, and Veeck was scolded. Two years later, his pocketbook was still bleeding. He sold Sportsman's Park to August Busch Jr., owner of the Cards, in 1953. The landlord was now the tenant, and Busch Stadium was born. By season's end, Veeck had sold his club to interests in Baltimore (where the franchise found far greater success as the Orioles).

Meanwhile, the Cards continued to flourish. Busch invested in the old ballpark, renovating the grandstand while reducing the venue's capacity to 30,500. He tried to name his park after his beer company, Budweiser, but the baseball lords weren't ready for corporate domination to be so shameless. Instead, he installed his company's trademark eagle above the left-center-field scoreboard; its wings flapped for every Cards homer. If the eagle didn't drive opponents crazy, Screechin' Screamin' Mary Ott, the "Horse Lady of St. Louis," did—for almost 25 years. The diehard fan made a name for herself by haranguing the opposition from her seat near the first-base dugout.

Sportsman's Park ended its run on May 8, 1966, when the Cards played their final game there before 17,503 nostalgic fans; the team's next stop was the modern confines of Busch Memorial Stadium. That same summer, Sportsman's Park came tumbling down.

Above: Sportsman's Park earned a rare distinction in 1944, hosting every game of that year's World Series. New York's Polo Grounds had been the only stadium to do so previously. *Left:* One of baseball's most memorable gimmicks took place at Sportsman's Park, where 3'7" stuntman Eddie Gaedel drew a pinch-hit walk in 1951 for gutsy Browns owner Bill Veeck.

GRIFFITH STADIUM: LAST IN THE AMERICAN LEAGUE

In our nation's capital, amid the array of cherry blossoms that arrive every spring, one tree stood out for Washington Senator fans. The phrase "Meet me by the tree" referred to the mighty oak that was anchored behind center field at Griffith Stadium.

The ballpark was actually built around this old oak and five houses, which contributed to the center-field fence dramatically jagging inward onto the outfield grass. Cynics would say the tree came first, something the Senators rarely did. Washington was a baseball town as far back as the Grant Administration. When the American League formed in 1901, Washington was included. League founder Ban Johnson bankrolled the team for its first three seasons. Its original home field was at 14th Street and Bladensburg Road NE. In 1903, the team moved to the former Boundary Field—a nondescript 10,000-seat facility that had hosted the National League's Washington

Above: The Griffith Stadium fan with this ducat saw baseball's best play in the 1956 All-Star Game. Willie Mays, Stan Musial, Ted Williams, and Mickey Mantle hit home runs in the contest, a 7–3 NL victory. *Right:* A massive oak tree and five nearby houses accounted for jutting center-field walls at Griffith Stadium, which served as home to some of baseball's least-competitive clubs.

Senators until that franchise folded in 1899—at Trinidad and Florida NE avenues. The AL club bestowed upon the facility a not-very-creative new name: American League Park.

What the ballpark lacked in style it made up for with doggone curiosity. In the deep regions of the outfield sat the grounds-crew doghouse, right next to a flagpole. Every day, the U.S. flag was taken down, folded and placed inside the tiny structure. Historian Philip J. Lowry, in his book *Green Cathedrals*, noted that one afternoon, the doghouse door was left open and a line drive wound up inside. It produced, at least according to Washington lore, baseball's only "inside-the-doghouse homer."

The park was noted for at least two innovations. Team employee E. Lawrence Phillips would announce the day's lineups over a megaphone—he was baseball's first public-address announcer. The venue saw the beginning of another tradition when President William Howard Taft heaved a ball from his grandstand seat to Walter Johnson, the Senators star pitcher, on Opening Day 1910. The presidential first pitch would be a celebrated event at Griffith Stadium through the John F. Kennedy presidency.

The following spring, with the Senators away at spring training, flames ripped through the run-down park, leaving essentially only a shell. In less than four weeks, with 800 workers alternating shifts around the clock, a new steel-and-concrete park rose from the ashes in time for Opening Day. The park would eventually grow into a double-deck venue that was noted for its expan-

sive outfield, which included a 30-foot concrete wall in right field. A scoreboard, which was just as hard on outfielders' bones, was affixed to the wall. At one time, a National Bohemian Beer ad—which featured a bottle that rose 56 feet into the air—dominated it. Home runs were rare: In 1945, for example, no Senator was able to hit one over the wall. It is said that only Yankee great Mickey Mantle and Negro League star Josh Gibson—whose team, the Homestead Grays, called the building home—managed to clear the left-field bleachers.

For most of their existence, the Senators were perennial losers, as duly noted by the quip attributed to Washington sportswriter Charles Dryden: "First in war, first in peace, last in the American League."

With the arrival of former pitcher Clark Griffith as manager in 1912, the team's fortunes changed, albeit briefly.

With Johnson, the "Big Train," hurling fastballs at unmatched speeds, they finished second in the AL two straight years. In 1920, Griffith bought the club, and the park was given his name; "The Old Fox" would remain in D.C. for four decades. In 1924, the Senators won the World Series. Another pennant followed the next season, and a third was captured in 1933.

Afterward, the Senators—never a financially sound organization—went into a 27-year pennantless slump. The team left Washington after the 1960 season, a year in which they finished fifth in the AL but last at the ticket window. An expansion team—also known as the Senators—took up residence at Griffith Stadium the following year before vacating to a new multipurpose park after the season. "Meet me at the tree" no longer had a meaning after January 26, 1965—the day Griffith Stadium came down.

The Senators finished last in the American League in attendance in each of their last six seasons at Griffith Stadium; they averaged less than 6,000 per home game in three of those years.

Chapter 3

EARLY EXPANSION

1933–1966

For five decades, baseball's role as America's national pastime was abandoned just beyond the banks of the Mississippi River. In subsequent years, however, baseball owners discovered untapped wealth in the West. This expansion gave rise to grand, even space-age, ballparks and stadiums. The nation finally embraced major-league baseball, from coast to coast.

Left: The expansion Mets may have struggled on the field, but they benefitted from playing at the huge Shea Stadium in Flushing, New York. *Above:* It's been a while since any major-league park could offer the kinds of ticket prices fans at Cleveland's Municipal Stadium enjoyed when this sign hung (probably the late 1970s).

Above: Though some considered Cleveland's Municipal Stadium to be the "mistake on the lake," no one could dispute its standing as one of the largest-capacity homes in the majors. *Right:* More than a baseball facility, Municipal Stadium hosted football, mini-car races, religious revivals, and scores of civic events. This keychain is a souvenir of the 57th Annual Shriners Convention, which occurred in 1931.

CLEVELAND MUNICIPAL: LAKEFRONT PROPERTY

No ballpark was more inviting than Cleveland's Municipal Stadium during games that drew full houses of 80,000. Problem was, unless it was Opening Day or the Indians were in a pennant chase (which was a rare occurrence), the place was often desolate.

It was a stadium the Indians didn't seem to want. For half of the 1932 season, the team put off playing their first game at the new multipurpose stadium, which was built atop an old landfill on

the shores of Lake Erie. Tribe owner Alva Bradley, who was still haggling with the city over the lease, preferred the handsome profits he gained at League Park, which the team owned and where it had played since its 1901 inception.

Finally, on July 31—with a baseball-record 80,284 on hand—the Indians played their first game at Municipal, a 1–0 loss to the A's. The next day, the Tribe drew an estimated 12,000. A trend had begun. The Indians stayed at the

Stadium through 1933 and then returned to League Park, using the behemoth on the lakefront only sporadically for special events through 1946.

Municipal Stadium's construction was an undertaking for civic leaders and taxpayers—it was the first publicly funded baseball facility—in the late 1920s. The horseshoe-shape stadium featured a massive double-deck grandstand that abutted a single-layer bleacher section in deep center field. When it first opened, home runs had to travel more than 470 feet to center and 322 feet down the lines.

"You'd have to have a horse to play outfield here," Babe Ruth once said.

The Stadium's glory years lasted from 1948 through 1959, when the Indians challenged the Yankees for the AL crown nearly every summer, winning two pennants and finishing second six times. The renaissance arrived in 1946 when Bill Veeck bought the Tribe and made Municipal Stadium his team's permanent home. During the Tribe's championship year of 1948, the team featured Hall of Famers Bob Feller, Lou Boudreau, Larry Doby, and Bob Lemon—and Veeck's legendary promotional gimmicks. That season, the Tribe set a record with 2.6 million spectators. A record crowd of 86,288 attended Game 5 of the World Series that fall.

A second pennant came in 1954, and a pennant chase followed in '59. Afterward, the team's fortunes sank—and so did fan interest. Low attendance meant low cash flow for team owners and scarce resources with which to scout and sign talent. Rumors of relocation dogged the city from the 1960s through the 1980s. Meanwhile, the Stadium was as lifeless as the baseball team. New paint and the addition of luxury loge seats attached to the upper deck did little for the old facility. Despite this, Gabe Paul, the team's president in the early 1970s, called the franchise a "sleeping giant." And indeed, signs of life would appear at times, such as in 1973, when 74,420 showed up for Opening Day. The next day, fewer than 11,000 attended.

Cleveland's fortunes changed in 1987, when developer Richard Jacobs bought the Indians and worked with civic leaders to persuade voters to once again help pay for a home for their woebegone Tribe. Municipal Stadium hosted its final Indians game on October 3, 1993, before a sold-out, nostalgic crowd. A jewel awaited them a few blocks south.

TINY LEAGUE PARK

LEAGUE PARK ORIGINALLY opened in 1891 for the National League's Cleveland Spiders; the venue also served as the Indians' original home. The Tribe played there (at least most of the time) from 1901 through 1946.

Jammed inside an East Side neighborhood, the park—after a renovation in 1910—featured a double-deck grandstand down each baseline. Right field offered players a 290-foot home-run porch that was created by a 40-foot fence blocking Lexington Avenue. Center field expanded dramatically to 505 feet. At its peak capacity, the park sat just over 21,000.

During the 1920 World Series, every seat—and then some—was needed, as the Indians beat the Dodgers. For Cleveland, Game 5 was magical. Second baseman Bill Wambsganss pulled off an unassisted triple play, Elmer Smith recorded the first-ever Series grand slam, and Jim Bagby rapped the first Series homer by a pitcher. The Indians left League Park for good following the 1946 campaign, after Bill Veeck bought the franchise.

Olympic sprinting champion Jesse Owens (left) beats speedy Cleveland outfielder George Case in a 100-yard dash exhibition across the outfield grass at Municipal Stadium in 1946.

THE PHILADELPHIA STORY: SHIBE PARK

The Great Depression delivered two things to Philadelphia's Shibe Park: the decline of the A's and the arrival of the Phillies. Somehow, baseball managed to survive in the city of Brotherly Love.

Connie Mack's Athletics won three AL pennants from 1929 to 1931, and by that time, Shibe Park—which was entering its third decade—had already undergone changes. After renovations in 1925, Shibe was nearly enclosed with doubled-deck stands (except in right field, where a 12-foot wall ran along 20th Street). A mezzanine was later added around the infield, giving the park seating for 33,000. In 1935, to finally end the freebie rooftop peeks from beyond right field, Mack ordered a 22-foot fence of corrugated sheet iron placed atop the wall. The structure was known as Mack's "spite fence."

Little else would change about the venerable park for the next 40 years—except the fortunes of the A's. Due to plummeting attendance, Mack was forced to move stars Mickey Cochrane and Lefty Grove in 1933, and Jimmie Foxx in 1935. The A's would never come close to contending for another pennant at Shibe.

The NL's Phillies, a perennial loser at the decrepit Baker Bowl, didn't fare much better after they moved to Shibe during the 1938 season. They didn't field a winner there until 1949, but in 1950, the "Whiz Kids" Phillies club captured the team's first pennant in 35 years. It was a fluke. Philadelphians were usually "blessed" with two lousy teams competing for dead last in their leagues in an aging park that was surrounded by a neighborhood in flux. Fans could not even have a beer, which was banned in the park for its first 52 years.

Mack sold the A's in 1954; the team's new owner promptly moved the franchise to Kansas City, ending the 17-year stadium-sharing arrangement. But the Phillies' woes continued. Symbolic of the team's empty pockets was a hand-me-down scoreboard from Yankee Stadium that was added in 1956. It was a monstrous 50-foot display that was slapped on the right-field wall; its most notable feature was a red-letter Ballantine Beer ad that sat atop it.

The Phillies, for better or worse, bought the ballpark in 1955 and stayed there through 1970. They played their final game at Shibe on October 1, 1970.

Top: Shibe Park went by the name "Connie Mack Stadium" beginning in 1953. This broadside advertises an interleague exhibition game held there in 1967. *Left:* The first major-league stadium constructed from steel and concrete, Shibe Park was a Philadelphia fortress that influenced dozens of other neighborhood stadium designs that followed.

MILWAUKEE'S COUNTY STADIUM BREWS UP FUN

Milwaukee rolled out the barrel for the Braves, and the Braves had a barrel of fun, thanks to the city's baseball-thirsty fans showering the team with a free stadium and its players with remarkable amenities.

Granted, County Stadium was no Taj Mahal—it had a spartan grandstand, a symmetrical field, and distant bleachers. But the ballpark was a trailblazer in one respect: It ushered in an era of cities building anticipation and stadiums for baseball despite not having teams. Ground was broken on the county-owned facility in 1950, three years before the Braves relocated from Boston, where the team's fortunes had long since floundered. It was major-league baseball's first franchise relocation in 50 years.

Milwaukee fans acted like bobby-soxers. The city had been without a team since 1901, so every Brave—from greats like Warren Spahn to journeymen like Andy Pafko—was offered free dinners, cheap gasoline, and discounted housing. More than 1.8 million fans passed through County Stadium's gates that first season. A National League-record two million came in 1954.

After four near misses, the Braves captured the NL pennant in 1957, with the heavy bat of Hank Aaron leading the way. In the World Series, the Braves clipped the Yankees in a thrilling seven-game showdown to capture the franchise's first championship since 1914. Another pennant came in '58, and second-place finishes followed in '59 and '60. But fans began to drift away as the team's fortunes subsequently declined. Another relocation came after the 1965 season, when the Braves moved to Atlanta.

County Stadium sat mostly empty for five seasons thereafter, except for a few Green Bay Packers NFL games per season and a handful of White Sox contests in 1968 and '69. But in 1970, Bud Selig bought the failing Seattle Pilots and created the Brewers, who took up residence at County. Fans were again engaged. Tailgate parties flourished. New bleachers pushed the park's capacity past 50,000. And in 1973, team mascot Bernie Brewer made his first slide into a faux beer mug after a Milwaukee home run. The fun lasted through 2000, after which the Brewers moved to nearby Miller Park. County Stadium was demolished in 2001.

Above: As this early 1950s postcard illustrates, there was nothing pretentious about Milwaukee's County Stadium, but players enjoyed the city's upper-Midwestern hospitality. *Left:* County Stadium's capacity stood at just over 36,000 when the park opened in 1953, but the accommodations grew to more than 43,000 within a year and swelled to 53,000-plus by the mid-1970s.

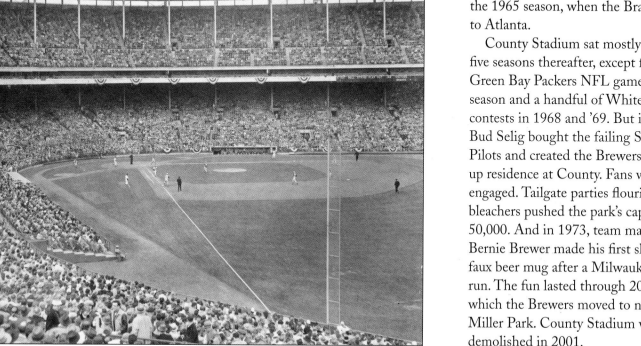

BALTIMORE'S GRAND OLD LADY

The Grand Old Lady of 33rd Street never looked so lovely. On April 15, 1954, Baltimore was welcomed back into the big leagues as the Orioles took the field at Memorial Stadium.

Baltimore's struggle to deliver that very first pitch in '54—which was tossed by Oriole right-hander Bob Turley—dated from 1903, when the city's original American League team bolted to New York, where it eventually became baseball's greatest dynasty. For years, Baltimore fans filed into Municipal Stadium to cheer the city's minor-league team (named the Orioles), which often outdrew other cities' major-league clubs. Fans knew that Baltimore should return to the big leagues.

Luckily, American League owners wanted St. Louis Browns' owner Bill Veeck out of baseball, and the league was poised to expand into uncharted cities. Veeck sold the Browns to buyers from Baltimore, and Charm City fans—whose tax dollars helped build Memorial Stadium—welcomed the major leagues.

Memorial Stadium had opened in 1950 to be home to the International League's Orioles; it later housed the city's NFL team, the Colts. Expansion of an uncovered upper deck that was added to suit the big-league Orioles was not completed by the 1954 season; lighting was also unfinished. At the main entrance off 33rd Street, amid Babe Ruth Plaza, rose the stadium's signature: a prominent facade that paid tribute to fallen soldiers. Inside, seating was expanded beyond 47,000, although

critics harped on the stadium's obstructive columns. Trees beyond the outfield provided a park-like setting. A grounds-keeper—and, later, Orioles players—tended a vegetable garden.

Memorial Stadium was originally a pitcher's park, with vast power alleys topping 445 feet. It took several seasons before the Orioles shook the losing tradition of the Browns, but by the mid-1960s, the team was a powerhouse, led by sluggers Brooks Robinson and Frank Robinson and pitching ace Jim Palmer. The O's won six pennants from 1966 to 1983, and captured World Series titles in 1966, '70, and '83. After the Colts bolted to Indianapolis in 1984, grumbling over

Memorial Stadium's shortcomings intensified. In 1992, the Orioles were on the move again, this time to Oriole Park at Camden Yards.

Right: This program and ticket stub are from the first major-league game at Municipal Stadium, a day that was a source of great pride in Baltimore. The Orioles landed with a parade and a 3–1 win over the White Sox. *Below:* Municipal Stadium was the first major-league park built entirely of reinforced concrete. Though some views were obstructed, fans there cheered the O's to six AL pennants and three World Series titles.

K.C.'S MUNICIPAL STADIUM SHAKES THE BLUES

Some fine players passed through the doors of the clunky ballpark at 22nd Street and Brooklyn Avenue in Kansas City—Satchel Paige, Jackie Robinson, and Mickey Mantle, for example. Whether through the minor-league Blues or the Negro American League Monarchs, Kansas City enjoyed a rich hardball tradition. But for many years, K.C. was a mere train stop for future Hall of Famers.

In 1955, however, the town entered the big leagues thanks to a handshake between Philadelphia Athletics owner Connie Mack and Kansas City business-man Arnold Johnson, who bought the team and moved it to Missouri. Although fans were ready, Kansas City's 22-year-old ballpark wasn't. Expanding antiquated Blues Stadium called for the addition of an upper deck, an engineering design that skeptics deemed impossible. With only four months before Opening Day, workers scrambled in unbearable winter conditions.

The inauguration went off without a hitch, as a Kansas City–record crowd of 32,844 welcomed the A's. The venue was renamed Municipal Stadium—at a cost of $500,000 to Johnson—and featured an outfield that fanned across a vast pasture. A double-deck grandstand stretched to the foul pole in right; archaic bleachers ran down the left-field line. A scoreboard that had been salvaged from Braves Field in Boston hung in right-center field.

After Johnson's death in 1960, the circus came to town in the form of eccentric, tightfisted new owner Charles O. Finley. The team was never successful while in Kansas City, but Finley tried to make it palatable. Believing that the Yankees owed their success to their shallow right-field wall, Finley created "Pennant Porch," a partitioned fence that sat 296 feet from home. It lasted for two exhibition games in 1964 before league officials ordered it to be taken down. Undaunted, Finley fashioned "One-Half Pennant Porch" 325 feet down the line.

Finley tried other gimmicks to draw fans to watch his weak clubs, but nothing worked. He packed up his carnival and moved it to Oakland in 1967. Baseball returned to Kansas City in 1969, however, with the expansion Royals. After four seasons at Municipal, though, the Royals left for the more refined setting of Royals Stadium. Muni Stadium was demolished in 1976.

Above left: Gimmicks such as an in-stadium petting zoo, a picnic area, and a mule mascot named "Charlie O" were among the bait for fans during years in which the A's struggled. *Above right:* Old Blues Stadium reopened in 1955 with an upper deck, a new name, and a relocated team, as fans turned out to see Enos Slaughter and the Kansas City Athletics.

THE MET IS RAISED ON PROMISES

Metropolitan Stadium near Minneapolis was raised on a cornfield of promises. Private investors constructed it in 1956 amid farmland in suburban Bloomington in the hope that a major-league team might find it suitable.

The Twin Cities waited five years before it drew a nibble, but the ballpark didn't sit empty: Exhibition-game auditions were held to attract the interests of antsy teams. In the meantime, the minor-league Minneapolis Millers helped fans pass the time until the promise of the big leagues was fulfilled.

Washington Senators owner Calvin Griffith was impressed by what he saw at the Met. And in 1961, after Minnesota met his demands of guaranteed attendance and other perks, he delivered his hapless Senators to the Twin Cities. His team was renamed the Minnesota Twins, a move designed to unite neighboring rivals Minneapolis and St. Paul. Minnesota fans knew that they were inheriting perennial losers. Under the Griffith family, the Senators had gone pennantless for nearly 30 years, and the defeats demoralized Washington fans. The club drew an AL-worst 743,404 during its last season in D.C.

For major-league-deprived fans in Minnesota, it didn't matter. Griffith quickly realized great profits, as attendance soared past 1.2 million in his team's first year at the Met. After an expansion in 1964, the structure boasted 40,000 seats in a curved triple-deck grandstand and bleachers that were located down the third-base line and beyond left field. Something else was about to change as well: The Twins were building a winner, led by an explosive offense featuring Harmon Killebrew and Tony Oliva.

By 1965, the Twins had surged to the top of the AL in both wins and attendance. While that year's Twins team lost to the Dodgers in a seven-game World Series, the club's success continued for several years: It notched division titles in 1969 and 1970.

But the Twins and the Met became also-rans as the 1970s unfolded. Never considered a treasure, the park was unkempt by major-league standards. The Twins played their last game at the Met on September 30, 1981. In 1985, it was demolished to make way for the mammoth Mall of America.

Metropolitan Stadium - Home of The Minnesota Twins and Vikings

Top: This field pass enabled the wearer to get close to the All-Stars in 1965. The Twins' Harmon Killebrew homered at his home field, though the American League ended up on the losing end of the game. *Above:* Once considered baseball's best minor-league stadium and a fine place for a football game, the Met—pictured here on an early 1960s postcard—joined the big leagues when the Twins came to town in 1961.

MID-1950S CALIFORNIA GOLD RUSH

Just like the prospectors who came to California during the Gold Rush, baseball expanded into the West in search of greater fortunes. This shift caused angst in New York, where the Giants and Dodgers left trails of disappointments on their paths to California. Both teams arrived for the 1958 season—the Giants at Seals Stadium in San Francisco and the Dodgers at the Los Angeles Memorial Coliseum. These ballparks were only temporary stops.

Seals Stadium had been home to the city's minor-league teams, one of which—the Seals—once included native son Joe DiMaggio. Set in a middle-class neighborhood, the ballpark's single-deck grandstand extended to the foul poles.

Willie Mays patrols the Seals Stadium outfield during the Giants' San Francisco debut. Mays drove in two runs in his team's 8–0 Opening Day win over the Dodgers on April 15, 1958.

Wooden bleachers in right field ended at a 31-foot-high center-field scoreboard. A prevailing wind was soaked with the aromas of a nearby bakery and brewery.

"There's nothing quite like the smell of new beer in the morning after a night on Frisco town," Giants pitcher Jim Brosnan wrote in his book *The Long Season*. The Giants left Seals Stadium for Candlestick Park after the 1959 season.

There was no baseball history at the Coliseum until the Dodgers made some. The multipurpose facility features more than 93,000 seats that fill a massive uncovered bowl—a stark contrast to the intimate Ebbets Field.

The Coliseum's conversion to a baseball field resulted in unused vastness and far-flung seats beyond a chain-link outfield fence. A notable aberration was a 42-foot left-field wall that stood a ridiculous 250 feet from home, over which slugger Wally Moon delivered his "Moon Shots." "I decided to shoot for the screen with what I call a calculated

slice," Moon said. The Dodgers made due, winning a World Series in 1959 while shattering attendance records. Their fans ranged from street cleaners to Hollywood celebrities. The Coliseum was overfilled on May 7, 1959, to salute Dodger catcher Roy Campanella, who had been paralyzed in a 1958 car crash. The Dodgers left the stadium after the 1961 season, but not for good: They returned in 2008 for an exhibition game against the Boston Red Sox that drew an uncanny 115,300.

It wasn't built for baseball, but the Los Angeles Coliseum could sure pack 'em in after the Dodgers arrived. Note the short left-field porch.

CANDLESTICK ENDURES GRUMBLES, RUMBLES

Rarely has a park garnered as much criticism as Candlestick Park. It's been dubbed "The North Pole" for its chilly air and "The Cave of the Winds" for the swirling breeze it creates off the San Francisco Bay.

The panning by the critics began soon after the stadium's first game, which took place on April 12, 1960, against the Cardinals. In several accounts of the contest, sportswriters opined that

Candlestick Park seemed to favor pitchers, unless a left-handed pull hitter was at the plate. The most striking storyline of the game, however, was that the wind was such a deciding factor. Giants left fielder Orlando Cepeda, a right-handed slugger known as "Baby Bull," was one of the first hitters to fall victim to the wind, as he saw a ball that he crushed die in the breeze and land in a Cardinal's glove. He knew, he said, that

he couldn't strike a ball harder than that particular hit. It was a different story in Candlestick's right field, where a wind tunnel jet-streamed balls off the bats of left-handed hitters.

The breezes at the 'Stick were legendary; so were the lawsuits that seemed to flutter in the Candlestick wind during the Giants' stay there. Legend has it that Giants owner Horace Stoneham agreed to the site after touring the bay's

Above: Its proximity to San Francisco Bay made Candlestick Park a picturesque setting for baseball, but the cold winds that came with it created problems for players and fans.

Candlestick Point during the morning, before the area's vexing winds would reveal themselves. One man, Charles Harney, owned the majority of the land, which made acquisition easy, as a voter-approved bond to finance construction was nearing its end.

Construction and design work were put in the hands of Harney and John Bolles, two men who would be building their first stadium. The results were predictable: Lawsuits and grand-jury investigations ensued over financing, cost overruns, and parking. Candlestick arose in time for Opening Day 1960, but problems emerged almost immediately. For example, a system that was to provide heat for half of the 42,553 seats was buried too deep in the concrete stands—it warmed nothing. Critics also seized on the park's design and location. The entire baseball world took notice of the winds during the 1961 All-Star Game, which was held at Candlestick, when Giants hurler Stu Miller was literally blown off the mound by a gust.

The Giants fared well at their new park, winning the National League pennant in 1962 before falling to the Yankees in the World Series. Superstar Willie Mays, who many feared would suffer in the winds of Candlestick, had one of his finest campaigns that year, socking 49 home runs. That season, the Giants led the circuit in hitting, ranked sixth in pitching, and, for the third straight season, finished second in attendance. Despite the team's success, the stadium needed work—critics said that a slope inherent at the site accelerated its deterioration. Indeed, more

than $16 million in renovations were made after just 11 seasons—a second deck was added and the 'Stick was enclosed to accommodate 59,000 spectators. Artificial turf and movable seats were included to better house the 49ers of the NFL. But the complaints didn't stop.

By 1989, however, the Giants were back in the World Series, this time playing their cross-bay rivals, the Oakland A's. It was supposed to be the "BART Series," in reference to the area's public transportation system. Instead, it will forever be remembered as the "Earthquake Series." Just prior to Game 3, a 7.1-magnitude earthquake rattled Candlestick. Shocked players hunted for their wives and children and sought refuge on the field. No one

was injured inside the stadium, although 67 people in the Bay Area were killed. The Series was delayed for ten days before Candlestick, which sustained only minor damage, was declared safe.

Over the years, efforts to publicly finance a new ballpark for the Giants failed, as voters rejected each proposal. Eventually, however, the team's ownership was able to privately fund a new facility, and following the 1999 season, the Giants set sail.

Left: Candlestick Park makes an appearance on this commemorative platter honoring the San Francisco Giants and their 1962 National League pennant, which was won with a sizzling 103–62 record. *Bottom:* Giants star Willie Mays presents the team's lineup card in front of a packed Candlestick Park on July 18, 1970, the day he registered his 3,000th career hit.

CHAVEZ RAVINE: A "PERFECT PARK"

Walter O'Malley's goal for his Los Angeles ballpark was rather simple: "I want to build the perfect park," the Dodgers owner asserted. Mission accomplished.

Over 50 years later, Dodger Stadium remains pristine—an enduring, fan-friendly ballpark that has been left largely untouched since its gates opened in 1962. It is baseball's third-oldest ballpark (behind Fenway Park and Wrigley Field), but it remains exactly what O'Malley envisioned decades ago. O'Malley was scouting Southern California locations for his ballpark from inside a helicopter when he spotted the perfect swath. Amid meager houses—with children, dogs, and goats running loose—he found his diamond in the rough hills of an area nicknamed "Chavez Ravine." The road to Opening Day, however, would be as bumpy as the distant San Gabriel Mountains.

There was land to buy, stubborn squatters to remove with cash or deputies, and legal claims to settle (the land had once been earmarked for public housing). O'Malley nearly went broke acquiring the 315 acres of real estate—Dodger Stadium was, after all, the first privately financed park since Yankee Stadium. Its price tag was at least $23 million, but "Taj O'Malley," as the facility has been called, exceeded even its owner's expectations.

In the 1950s, America's love affair with the automobile was in full swing. More and more highways were paved as Americans headed for the suburbs. O'Malley recognized this shift—his ballpark was built with its customers in mind, featuring easy highway access, nearby parking for 16,000 cars, wide concourses, and open concession stands that offer Dodger Dogs and views of the diamond. There is nary a bad spot in the 56,000-seat venue.

Dodger Stadium presents views of mountain peaks and palm trees beyond center field and a wave of pastel seats that unfurl over five decks. The ballpark accommodates the diverse Los Angeles population; it initially offered everything from $1.50 general admission seats to a field-level dugout loge suitable for the rich and famous (a concept O'Malley borrowed from Japan). Dodger Stadium is known as baseball's cleanest park—it's meticulously washed and freshly painted

Above left: For four years, beginning in 1962, the Dodgers and Angels shared Dodger Stadium as their home turf, as Walter Alston and Bill Rigney point out on this poster. The Angels moved to Anaheim Stadium in 1966. *Left:* Fans arrived early to Dodger Stadium on April 10, 1962. Though their team lost to Cincinnati, most left raving about the sparkling new facility.

every off-season. But it wasn't exactly perfect that first season: The foul poles were askew and completely in foul territory, and drinking fountains were somehow left out of the design. Plans to provide a center-field fountain and enclose the park to expand seating to 85,000 never developed.

From 1962 to '65, Dodger Stadium also served as home to the expansion Los Angeles Angels, an American League club that was owned by Hollywood cowboy Gene Autry. The Angels failed to find a fan base in Chavez Ravine, however, and relocated to Anaheim for the 1966 campaign.

Dodgers fans, however, responded at the gates to the tune of 2.7 million attendees that first season, and the team returned the favor on the diamond. After finishing second in the NL in 1962, the Dodgers swept the Yankees in the World Series in 1963. Manager Walter Alston's team was built on pitching, speed, and defense, taking full advantage of Dodger Stadium's deep symmetrical outfield. Few teams could counter the Dodgers' one-two pitching combination of Sandy Koufax and Don Drysdale or the record-setting fleetness of shortstop Maury Wills. Dodger Stadium's prestige only grew as more

pennants and record-shattering attendance followed in ensuing years.

O'Malley turned over daily operations of the team to his son, Peter, just before the 1970 season, but he stayed on as chairman until his death nine years later. Both former owner Frank McCourt and current ownership group Guggenheim Baseball Management launched massive renovation projects that have spiffed up the stadium over the last decade, including the unveiling of hexagonal video boards in 2013. "It's not just for the fans," McCourt told the *Los Angeles Times* of his 2008 renovations. "It's for the entire community."

Dodger Stadium, nestled in the hills of Chavez Ravine, hosted eight World Series in its first 27 years as home of the Dodgers. Los Angeles won half of those titles.

THE EIGHTH WONDER OF THE WORLD

Though fans could count on air-conditioned protection from the hot Houston summers, baseball traditionalists were not sold on the "Eighth Wonder of the World."

Because of its engineering ingenuity, it was dubbed the "Eighth Wonder of the World." But many who ventured inside the Astrodome wondered why in the world it was built. Houston heat, mosquitoes, and the brains of a flamboyant millionaire made the Astrodome a reality, but rarely has a stadium been so roundly ridiculed in baseball circles.

For three seasons, the Houston Colt .45s and their fans sweated and swatted their way through summers at Colt Stadium. Everything is bigger in Texas, and that includes the mosquitoes—"twin-engine jobs," as Dodgers ace

Sandy Koufax recalled. The owner of the Colt .45s, Roy Hofheinz, decided that the obvious solution was taking his team indoors. It was a notion that he first explored for a geodesic-dome shopping mall and was reinforced by a visit to the Colosseum in Rome, which Hofheinz learned was once roofed.

Traditionalists immediately scoffed at the idea of the Astrodome. But Hofheinz pursued his vision—all 18 stories of it—at a cost to taxpayers of $31 million. When it was unveiled in 1965, optimists marveled at its sheer size; ballplayers, on the other hand, winced.

A major design flaw revealed itself during exhibition games: The dome's translucent ceiling created a glare so intense that seeing a flying baseball was nearly impossible. Hofheinz offered sunglasses to outfielders, some of whom donned batting helmets to protect their noggins. Before Opening Day, Hofheinz bowed to the pressure and had an acrylic coating splashed on the roof. It killed the glare—and the dome's natural grass. A year later, Houston introduced a game-changing "innovation" that shaved years off the careers of generations of players: artificial turf, dubbed "Astroturf."

Left: Senators outfielder Frank Howard practices locating an airborne baseball against the distraction of the Astrodome roof before the 1968 All-Star Game. *Above:* The 390-foot distance to the Astrodome's power alleys was the longest in the majors until 1985, when the fences were brought in to give sluggers a fighting chance.

The Astrodome—so-called in reference to its space-age design—did provide some unheard-of luxuries and odd quirks. Fans were treated to an air-conditioned climate free of pests, and an exploding scoreboard lit up for those rare Astro home runs that managed to escape the dome's artificial air and deep fences. No one in the building was more comfortable than Hofheinz, whose suite included a barbershop and a bowling alley. His rent at the dome, for his team and suite, was a mere $750,000 a year.

Despite its warts, the Astrodome became a fixture of the American sports scene. The NFL's Houston Oilers called it home from 1968 to 1996. The University of Houston basketball team played UCLA there in the "Game of the Century" in 1968, nearly 53,000 saw

Cougars star Elvin Hayes lock horns with Bruins sensation Lew Alcindor that day. And, in 1973, the made-for-TV "Battle of the Sexes" pitted tennis great Billie Jean King against self-promoter Bobby Riggs inside the Astrodome. But after the 1999 season, the Astros moved on to Enron Field. With no major tenants, the Astrodome still stands, as the city of Houston has been unable to decide what to do with it. In 2005, more than 25,000 evacuees from Hurricane Katrina-ravaged New Orleans called the Astrodome home for a short while.

COLT STADIUM

COLT STADIUM WAS, in the words of critics, the only ballpark in which bug spray outsold beer. There was one positive aspect to the marriage of Houston's expansion franchise to the facility, however: It was only a short-term deal. While the Astrodome was being built next door, the Colt .45s played in this one-deck stopgap, which had been built in a swamp.

If it wasn't the tortuous heat that ate at fans, it was the flurry of mosquitoes that infiltrated Colt Stadium every day. During one game, 100 fans suffered heat-related symptoms. Between innings, workers sprayed insect repellent in a never-ending battle with the bugs. Yet somehow, the Colts drew more than 924,000 fans in 1962, the team's first season. Perhaps it was to hear a young public address announcer named Dan Rather. Or maybe it was for the Hell Fire Stew that was served at the Fast Draw Club.

The pain for fans ended as intended after three seasons. In the '70s, the stands were dismantled and moved more than 350 miles south for a Mexican League franchise in Gomez Palacio.

THE KING OF QUEENS

It was under the watch of Mayor Robert F. Wagner Jr. that forlorn New Yorkers saw their beloved but tightfisted Giants and Dodgers bolt town during the dark autumn of 1957. Left with two obsolete and empty ballparks, Wagner was determined to bring a National League team back to the Big Apple. Really, he had little choice: He was up for re-election. To bolster his poll numbers, Wagner commissioned a panel to secure a new franchise. Bill Shea was Wagner's confidant, attorney, and hired gun.

"Families go to ballparks and that is why baseball is still our national game," Shea said.

Rumors about the relocation of established franchises from Cincinnati, Philadelphia, or Pittsburgh abounded; all failed to fold under Shea's pressure. Major League Baseball, however, crumbled under Shea's threat to create the Continental League, which was slated to begin play in 1961. New York was granted an MLB expansion franchise for 1962, but Shea should've held out for a *good* team: The

Mets were horrible that first season—and so was the Polo Grounds, their home field. The presence of the legendary Casey Stengel, the Mets aging manager, softened the blow of losing 120 games that season. Things improved the following year: The Mets lost just 111 games.

While the Mets were busy becoming lovable losers, Wagner's underlings were busy building a new ballpark on Flushing Bay, a former marsh and garbage dump. Worker strikes and brutal winters in 1962 and '63 delayed the park's opening.

Named after its aggressive suitor, Shea Stadium was inaugurated in April 1964; it sat alongside the World's Fair and below the thunderous jets that roared to and from LaGuardia Airport. The circular four-deck grandstand with 55,000 colored seats ran to the foul poles, allowing for an open view (mostly of parked cars) beyond the outfield fences. Two movable stands set on railroad tracks were included in the design to provide better views when the stadium was configured for football. A grand scoreboard that displayed color player photos was located beyond the right-field wall. Four restaurants served up meals. Jane Jarvis, the "Melody Queen of Shea Stadium," began her 15-year run of serenading fans from the ballpark's organ. More than 1.7 million showed up to watch another last-place finish that season. "Anybody can come out and see us, women, men and children, because we got 50 bathrooms all over the place," Stengel marveled.

In each of their first seven seasons, the Mets finished either last or next-to-last. But 1969 turned the baseball world upside down: the Amazin' Mets won the NL pennant, the World Series, and the hearts of many New Yorkers.

Over the years, Shea saw more miracles, including another pennant in 1973 and an improbable comeback in the '86 World Series that led to victory over the hard-luck Red Sox. In 2000, the Mets revisited the New York rivalries of the 1950s when they faced the Yankees in the Fall Classic. Shea Stadium fell quiet after the 2008 season, when the Mets moved across the parking lot into their new home, Citi Field. Shea was razed in the winter of 2009. During a final farewell ceremony, some of the greatest Mets paid tribute.

Top left: This pennant celebrates the 1964 All-Star Game, which was held at Shea Stadium. The Mets' Ron Hunt started at second base for the National League. The contest was a thriller—Johnny Callison's walk-off homer won it for the NL, 7–4. *Left:* Do you believe in miracles? Shea Stadium patrons did in 1969, when they celebrated their "Miracle Mets" and a stunning World Series win over Baltimore.

The wrecking ball does its work on the Polo Grounds 1964; it is the same one that had been used on Ebbets Field in 1960.

THE POLO GROUNDS' LAST HURRAH

THERE WAS A reason the Giants left the Polo Grounds; actually, there were many reasons. After five decades, the once-grand ballpark was weary and its neighborhood downtrodden. The stadium's decline only worsened when the Mets arrived in 1962 for what everyone knew was a short-term engagement. The team seemed to be as run-down as its ballpark.

Casey Stengel's club left with haste after the final out in a 5–1 loss to the Phillies on September 18, 1963, which was played before just 1,752 fans. Despite all the history the Polo Grounds had seen, there was no ceremony, no nostalgia. In fact, it was the smallest gathering ever for a Mets game at the stadium. In April 1964, workers wearing Giants jerseys took a wrecking ball—the very one that had been used on Ebbets Field in 1960—to the old ballyard, finishing the task that time and neglect had begun. In its place arose a group of 30-story apartment buildings.

Chapter 4

THE MODERN AGE

1966–1988

Baseball's success led the game to spread across the nation and even into Canada, but it did so at the expense of the fan experience. As the major leagues proliferated to new cities, aging and inadequate ballparks were replaced with taxpayer-funded multipurpose stadiums. History would be unkind to these edifices.

Left: Royals Stadium in Kansas City, now known as Kauffman Stadium, is instantly recognizable due to its crown-shape scoreboard and picturesque water displays that draw attention beyond the outfield walls. *Above:* Those instrumental in bringing big-league baseball to Canada put their signatures on a commemorative ball on August 14, 1968, when the Expos were admitted to the National League.

THE PROTOTYPICAL COOKIE CUTTER: RFK STADIUM

In 1962, Calvin Griffith and his Washington Senators could have had a new state-of-the-art ballpark, complete with movable grandstands and modern seats. The facility—D.C. Stadium—was being built, but Griffith wasn't up for the continued struggle in the nation's capital. Instead, he took his club and its long history and headed for the unchallenged market of Minnesota. Someone else would have to go forward with the "Beltway Battle" against the Baltimore Orioles, who played just 40 miles away from Washington.

Born from Griffith's shift of his club was an expansion team for Washington; this new franchise was also called the Senators. It was a prearranged deal—baseball owners were engaged in an antitrust battle, which meant that the leagues had to expand.

The Beltway Battle had raged since 1954, when Clark Griffith (the longtime Senators owner and former manager) signed off on the St. Louis Browns' move to Baltimore, foregoing any territorial concerns. Of course, financial considerations from a Baltimore beer company, enhanced broadcast rights, and plenty of cash helped seal the deal. After Clark Griffith died in 1955, his succes-sor, Calvin Griffith, decided to concede his uncle's territorial struggles.

The new Senators played the 1961 season at old Griffith Stadium. Awaiting them in 1962 was D.C. Stadium, the only federally owned ballpark in the country. It was a far cry from the team's diminutive former home, and not for the right reasons. Yes, it had that "new ballpark" smell and was grand in scale, offering seating for 45,000 fans. But D.C. Stadium was also the first of the so-called "cookie cutter" stadiums that were built to house both baseball and football, sports with grossly incompatible playing dimensions. For fans of the Washington Redskins of the NFL, the stadium was spectacular; to baseball enthusiasts, however, it had distant seats and a lack of intimacy. Even with its movable grand-stands, the conversion from baseball field to football field was complicated enough to cost $40,000 to execute each time the change was made.

The stadium was poorly received, and the Senators were equally hard to watch. Attendance during that first season averaged less than 10,000 a game, and the Senators lost 100 or more games during of their first four years of exis-tence. Meanwhile, the Twins were chasing pennants, and across the Beltway, the O's were crafting a dynasty.

In 1969, the stadium was renamed Robert F. Kennedy Memorial Stadium in honor of the slain New York senator. But

Above: A metal sign removed from Washington's RFK Stadium touts cheap seats to Senators games, though some who followed the club's struggles might have cringed even at this price. *Right:* President John F. Kennedy throws out the ceremonial first pitch from the stands at D.C. Stadium on Opening Day 1962, when the park debuted as the home of the Washington Senators.

by 1971, the "new" Senators had worn out their welcome in D.C. Never had they finished higher than fourth place nor drawn a million fans in a season. Fans despised owner Bob Short for refusing to invest in his team.

Frustrations overflowed on September 30, 1971, during the Senators' final game at RFK before their move to Arlington, Texas. With two outs in the ninth and the Senators holding a 7–5 lead over the Yankees, some of the 14,460 fans who bothered to show up poured onto the

field, prompting umpires to forfeit the game to New York.

The city failed to obtain a major-league franchise during expansions in 1993 and 1998, but baseball returned to the nation's capital in 2005, when the struggling Montreal Expos relocated and became the Washington Nationals. The move didn't come without a fight, however, as concerns were again voiced over two teams sharing the market's more than eight million residents. This time, the cries came from Orioles management, which

had enjoyed exclusivity for over 30 years. In recent times, both the Orioles and Nats have suffered at the gate, as fears of a split fan base appear to have been realized. The failures of both teams in the standings hasn't helped to sell tickets, either.

"This is an enormous market and a rich market—the team just isn't where it needs to be," said Nationals' president Stan Kasten.

The Nationals spent three seasons at RFK before moving into their new stadium, Nationals Park.

Major-league baseball returned to RFK Stadium in 2005 after a 33-year hiatus, but it was a short engagement. Here, fans attend the park's final homestand in 2007.

BUSCH CROWNS THE CONCRETE DOUGHNUT

While the Cardinals were on their way to a World Series triumph in 1964, St. Louis construction workers were building a new throne for the National League's kings.

Sportsman's Park, the Cards' home since 1920, was hardly an appropriate castle. Cosmetic changes made by owner August Busch Jr.—fresh crimson, jade, and blue paint, for example, and the addition of green center-field shrubbery—only covered so much of time's torment.

Meanwhile, downtown St. Louis was undergoing its own revitalization, and the Cards' new ballpark and the Gateway Arch (which rose eight blocks away) served as its cornerstones. On May 12, 1966, a short time after home plate was delivered by helicopter from Sportsman's, Busch Stadium opened with a Cards win over Atlanta before a crowd of 46,048. Although its circular shell was similar to those of the much-maligned "concrete doughnut" stadiums of the decade, Busch Stadium was somehow different. With 96 arches crowning the stadium, it fit nicely with the nearby Gateway Arch. The shadows cast onto the stadium's natural grass field by these rooftop arches from 130 feet in the air reminded everyone that they were in St. Louis.

With room for 50,000, Busch Stadium gave its owner nearly 50 percent more tickets to sell than did Sportsman's Park. And Cards' fans responded. In fact, never in the stadium's history did the team draw fewer than a million spectators in a season.

The Cardinals shared the facility with the city's NFL team (which bore the same nickname), and the annual conversion from a baseball diamond to a football field took its toll on the natural playing surface. In response, Astroturf, the new-wave plastic grass, was rolled onto the outfield in 1970; seven years later, the entire playing field was covered with the fake stuff. Thanks to the rug, Redbirds baseball changed: Grounders ripped past infielders, balls bounced over outfielders' heads, and the St. Louis summer heat seemed more scorching.

To suit their stadium, the Cardinals built a team based on speed, defense, and pitching. "I became more of a slap hitter in this park because the ballpark sort of dictated it," said Cards Hall of Famer Lou Brock.

Above: Nothing says "St. Louis" quite like the magnificent Gateway Arch towering above Busch Stadium. This shot was taken during the 1966 All-Star Game, which was played in the midst of a scalding heat wave. *Right:* Busch Stadium hosted the World Series in two of its first three years of existence, and it had a prominent place on this ticket. The Cardinals defeated the Red Sox in 1967 and lost to the Tigers in 1968.

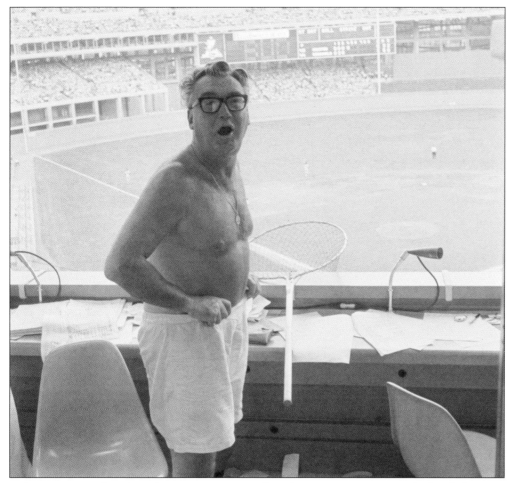

Holy Cow! Legendary broadcaster Harry Caray found an interesting way to deal with the sweltering heat and humidity of Busch Stadium—he called a Cardinals game in his underwear in 1966.

After the departure of the football Cardinals in 1987, Busch Stadium became a baseball-only facility, and in 1996, real grass was tromped on within its confines once again. A retro hand-operated scoreboard was installed the following year. Organist Ernie Hays played on, leading the crowd with the Budweiser theme "Here Comes the King," as well as the traditional "Take Me Out to the Ballgame."

A slugger named Mark McGwire brought more changes to Busch. Mac single-handedly made the ballpark a launching pad—he collected 38 of his then-record 70 home runs in 1998 at home. The Redbirds' run at Busch ended in 2005. During a nearly two-hour ceremony, former Cardinal players from the 1960s and onward took their positions and saluted their fans. A new ballpark that was rising next door beckoned.

THE CARDINALS HALL OF FAME MUSEUM

How many buildings had a sweaty ball cap, a '62 'Vette, and a portrait of "Stan the Man" under one roof? Just one: The St. Louis Cardinals Hall of Fame Museum. The walk-through history gallery opened beneath Busch Stadium in 1968 and featured homages to some of the greatest moments and characters in St. Louis's illustrious baseball history dating back to the 19th century.

For years, fans could eye memorabilia from the Cards and Browns, as well as other St. Louis baseball artifacts. These items included reliever Steve Kline's filthy cap from 2001 (when he appeared in 89 games), the Corvette given to slugger Mark McGwire in honor of his home-run record, and tributes to the great Cardinals of the past, from Stan Musial to Ozzie Smith. It also contained the Cards' championship trophies from 1967 and 1982, as well as historic jerseys, baseballs, and artwork. The museum went on hiatus in 2008; it reopened in 2014 across the street from the new Busch Stadium in the St. Louis Ballpark Village.

This Gold Glove Award won by Ozzie Smith in 1986 was one of 13 that he won during his career.

THE BIG A: ANAHEIM STADIUM

Like a couple of Hollywood movie stars, Angel Stadium and the team that calls it home, the Los Angeles Angels, have reinvented themselves. Both were once unassuming and unpolished, but they are now among the finest in baseball.

Since Anaheim Stadium opened in 1966, it has transformed from a nondescript baseball-only venue to a multipurpose facility and back. It is now one of baseball's most inviting ballparks.

The Angels descended into major-league baseball in 1961 with a Hollywood owner, "quintessential good guy" Gene Autry. Their first season was spent at Wrigley Field, a minor-league park at 42nd Place and Avalon Boulevard in south-central Los Angeles that has been once owned by the same chewing-gum company that owned the Cubs. Beginning in 1962, the Angels became tenants at Dodger Stadium for four seasons.

Walt Disney is credited with steering Autry to Anaheim. It was there that Autry bought 148 acres of farmland that had produced alfalfa, corn, and eucalyptus and orange trees. In the early 1960s, Anaheim was a burgeoning suburb, as carloads of families were drawn to the Disneyland amusement park. Mickey Mouse and his gang helped promote the ballpark's groundbreaking. The Angels' new $24-million home was located two miles away from the "happiest place on Earth" and ready for the 1966 season.

The ballpark was easy to find from three different freeways; all one had to do was look for the 23-story "A" with a halo circling its top. The "A" was propped beyond left field and served as a stadium landmark, scoreboard, and advertising

Above: Angels Stadium of Anaheim has undergone multiple facelifts and name changes in its history, but it has remained a favorite of fans who want to soak up baseball and Southern California sunshine.

placard, all for $1 million. The sign gave the stadium its nickname: "The Big A."

Anaheim Stadium originally held 43,000 spectators in a rounded, three-deck grandstand that ended in the rolling bluegrass outfield, providing a view of parked cars and the San Gabriel Mountains in the distance. While there were no outfield seats, there also were no obstructed sight lines. There were, however, plenty of runs, as the ballpark quickly earned a reputation as a hitter's haven. Before the franchise moved into the park, Autry changed his team's name from the "Los Angeles Angels" to the "California Angels," a switch that reflected not only the team's new address but its desire to broaden its fan base.

The park's first transformation came in 1979, when the stadium was totally enclosed to offer expanded seating for the NFL's Los Angeles Rams; unfortu-

nately, this move tainted Anaheim Stadium's quaintness as a baseball facility. As part of the renovation, the "Big A" sign was wheeled into the parking lot. The Rams left for St. Louis in 1995, however, so in the late 1990s, the stadium underwent a magnificent $118-million facelift that remade it as a baseball-only facility with seating for about 45,000. Under the ownership of The Walt Disney Company, the ballpark again became inviting, as the outfield sky view returned and a new retro facade welcomed patrons. Included in the amusement-park-style design is the "Outfield Extravaganza," which features waterfalls and a geyser that shoots fireworks surrounded by imitation boulders that are designed to reflect the California coastline.

From 1997 to 2003, the park was renamed Edison International Field, thanks to the energy company's $50-million naming-rights agreement. At around the same time, the team changed its name to the "Anaheim Angels." In 2002, the Angels won their first World Series.

In late 2003, under new owner Arte Moreno, the ballpark was renamed Angel Stadium; after the following season, the team was dubbed the "Los Angeles Angels of Anaheim." Moreno quickly endeared himself to fans, three million of whom came to Angel Stadium in his first season. Not only did he finance a top-flight team, he lowered ticket and concession prices. "If I have a stadium 90 percent full of kids, then I'm a happy guy," he told *USA Today*.

Above: The diamond-shape patio area at the main entrance to Angel Stadium of Anaheim provides shade with two giant Angels hats. *Left:* Anaheim's ballpark wasn't nicknamed "The Big A" for Angels owner Gene Autry, but rather for its 23-story, halo-topped scoreboard. The landmark was moved to the parking lot in 1980.

COOKIE CUTTERS AND CONCRETE DOUGHNUTS

Cookie cutters, concrete doughnuts—whatever you call the multipurpose ballparks that began to rise in the 1960s, they have come to symbolize baseball's Dark Ages, a period of 30 years in which just one stadium was built for baseball only. Virtually indistinguishable and uninviting, these structures cropped up from coast to coast—in Atlanta, Philadelphia, Pittsburgh, Cincinnati, St. Louis, and Oakland.

These monstrosities were super-size and round, inside and out—a necessity for housing both baseball and football, as well as any traveling show that may come to town. During this period, taxpayers were the only folks who paid for stadiums, and politicians looked to maximize the public's steep investments. In most cases, the fields were symmetrical look-alikes that were covered with artificial turf—sans the patches of brown dirt around the bases, home plate, and the pitcher's mound, of course.

Besides appearance, nearly all of the concrete bowls share another nuance: Although initially billed as modern, space-age achievements in stadium construction, most have already been beaten down by the wrecking ball.

Atlanta-Fulton County Stadium symbolized the trend. It was built in 50 weeks in the mid-1960s to lure professional sports franchises to the expanding southern city. The Braves arrived from Milwaukee in 1966, one year after the stadium opened. The facility sat about 52,000 for baseball, but due to its circular design, many seats were far from the action, eliminating the close connections between fans and players that defined early ballparks. In 1969, the Braves won

the first NL West division title, and power-hitting Hank Aaron was well on his way to eclipsing Babe Ruth's all-time home-run record. Aaron's game was spurred by the stadium's high elevation, which gave rise to its "Launching Pad" nickname that referred to all the home runs that shot over its walls, and not just by "Hammerin' Hank." Aaron, Darrell Evans, and Davey Johnson each clubbed 40 or more home runs in 1973.

History came to the stadium on April 8, 1974 (Opening Night), when Hammerin' Hank hit homer No. 715 to pass the Babe. Afterward, the Braves went into a tailspin and attendance dwindled. Promotions such as "Headlock and Wedlock Night," in which marriages and pro wrestling collided, failed to spur much activity. A game in 1976 attracted only 970 fans. In 1997, the stadium was deemed useless and was demolished.

In 1966, on the opposite coast, Oakland-Alameda County Coliseum opened for the Raiders of the American Football League. It wasn't meant for the A's, but nevertheless, they called it home after arriving from Kansas City for the 1968 season. Despite the wacky promotions of owner Charles O. Finley and three straight World Series titles in the early 1970s, Athletics attendance was simply awful. The stadium's foul territory is expansive, and the distance between the fans and the field of play is symbolic. Things only worsened when the Raiders returned from a 14-year stay in Los Angeles and demanded that more seats be added; in 1996, the view beyond the outfield was replaced with a towering grandstand. Efforts by the A's to per-

suade the city to build a baseball-only facility have consistently failed.

In 1970, Cincinnati and Pittsburgh opened nearly identical ballparks along the Ohio River. Neither was ready for Opening Day, but ironically, the NL Championship Series that fall would pit the teams and their new stadiums against each other.

Riverfront Stadium still wasn't complete when it opened with a Reds–Braves tilt on June 30. For some, attending a game there meant parking in Covington, Kentucky, and walking across the John A. Roebling Bridge to Ohio. Riverfront was a far cry from Crosley Field.

Above: Pittsburgh's Three Rivers Stadium was home not only to the Pirates' 1971 and '79 World Series winners, but to the Pittsburgh Steelers' football dynasty. *Right:* Willie Stargell, Dave Parker, and the rest of the title-winning Pirates sang "We Are Family" in 1979, and a Three Rivers Stadium banner welcomed fans as part of their extended family clan.

Although it offered modern amenities that Crosley didn't, Riverfront's grass was fake and its seating distant. The Reds, however, rose above the criticism of their home. The "Big Red Machine" of the 1970s was a true dynasty; led by hit king Pete Rose and two-time MVP Joe Morgan, the Reds played in four World Series in the stadium's first seven seasons. By 2002, however, Riverfront was a relic. "It rounded third and headed headlong into home," Reds announcer Joe Nuxhall said as the stadium was demolished on December 29 of that year.

Three Rivers Stadium opened on July 16, 1970, as the Pirates left endearing but outmoded Forbes Field. Built on the exact site of the 19th century's Exposition Park, Three Rivers was initially hailed by Pittsburgh fans for its sleek enormity, convenience, and bright lights. They arrived by car, bus, boat, and on foot via the Sixth Street Bridge. And the Pirates responded with six division titles and two World Series championships in their first decade in the stadium. But by the mid-1990s, Three Rivers had outlived its usefulness. Much of the upper-deck seating was covered and closed, as the by-then-hapless Pirates rarely needed all 48,000 seats. After the Pirates left for PNC Park following the 2000 season, Three Rivers was eulogized for hosting Pittsburgh triumphs. As a ballpark, however, it was panned. "It was ugly, lousy for watching baseball and surrounded by a dead sea of asphalt," wrote the editors of the *Pittsburgh Tribune-Review*.

In Philadelphia, the Phillies eagerly departed Shibe Park, which by 1971 was beyond life-support despite once being crowned the game's palace. Veterans Stadium, which was built in South Philly alongside the Spectrum arena and John F. Kennedy Stadium, was the last of the concrete doughnuts, though with its square shape and rounded corners, it more closely resembled a gray Long John. The taxpayer-funded venue cost $50 million, making it one of the most expensive facilities to date.

Above left: This sign took a beating on the outfield wall at Veterans Stadium, where it was hung to commemorate the 1983 pennant-winning Phillies club that was led by Mike Schmidt and Steve Carlton. *Left:* It wasn't built for baseball, and Oakland Coliseum has rarely been full for the A's, despite the four World Series crowns and six AL pennants the team has won in the facility.

"Cookie-cutter" though it might have been, Atlanta-Fulton County Stadium hosted Hank Aaron's record-setting 715th home run in 1974, along with the outset of the Braves' pitching-powered 1990s juggernaut.

Of all the ballparks of the cookie-cutter generation, the Vet was perhaps the most maligned. Its upper deck was ridiculously far from the field, thanks largely to the inclusion of 23 luxury suites that circled the grandstand. When it opened, the stadium sat more than 56,000, but on the field the Phillies remained a struggling franchise. The team's fortunes changed after a few seasons at the Vet; starting in 1976, the Phillies won their first of three straight division titles. Four years later, in 1983, they won the franchise's first-ever World Series championship.

The Vet was harshly criticized for its artificial turf, which sported dangerous seams and water stains. It was shuttered following the 2003 season, but despite its blemishes, the closing of Veterans Stadium, much like the expirations of its cousins, brought forth emotions from fans. It's the memories that played out at the Vet that matter most.

ASTROTURF AND THE RUNNING GAME

WHEN THEY ROLLED out the rug at the Astrodome, groundskeepers grabbed vacuums and ballplayers donned running shoes.

Love it or hate it, artificial turf changed baseball when it arrived in 1965. Balls shot through infields and bounced high off the carpeted concrete. The game became faster. Multi-purpose stadiums could be transformed almost instantly.

After the Houston experiment, Monsanto Industries' rug became known as "AstroTurf" and other cities adopted it. In 1969, the White Sox organization installed the fake stuff in Comiskey Park's infield. Candlestick Park, Busch Stadium, and Riverfront Stadium came next. Three Rivers Stadium in Pittsburgh utilized 3M's version, Tartan Turf; Kansas City followed suit soon after. The Reds, Royals, Phillies, and Cards won with speed over power, but aching knees cut many turf-bound careers short.

Today, artificial turf remains at two baseball parks: Rogers Centre in Toronto and Tropicana Field in St. Petersburg, both of which use a cushioned, realistic-looking artificial surface called "FieldTurf," which was designed in the 1990s by Tarkett Sports.

The Astrodome grounds crew donned spacesuits to tidy up the AstroTurf field.

OH CANADA: MONTREAL AND TORONTO

No-frills Jarry Park increased its seating capacity almost tenfold when it served as a stopgap between the Expos' debut in 1969 and the construction of a new stadium.

As far back as 1890, baseballs shot across the sometimes-frozen tundra of Montreal. Finally, in 1969, the expansion Expos brought major-league ball to the Great White North.

Jarry Park was oversold and aflutter on Opening Day in 1969, when the Expos hosted the defending National League-champion Cardinals in the first regular-season major-league game played outside the United States. Expos outfielder Mack Jones marked the historic occasion with a first-inning three-run homer that helped power Montreal to an 8–7 win.

Not long before, *Parc Jarry* was part of a neighborhood recreation center, catering to the friends and families of local sandlot heroes and seating 3,000. A quick overhaul extended an uncovered single-deck grandstand to each foul pole. Bleacher seats sat isolated beyond left field, giving Jarry Park room for 28,500, all told.

These were unquestionably austere digs, but they were only temporary; a dome stadium had been pledged when Montreal was granted an expansion team. However, two years in Jarry Park (as was promised) turned into more than seven. Yet these spartan confines suited the rag-tag Expos just fine.

"The place had a buzz," said Expo reliever Claude Raymond, a Montreal native, who had played as a teen in old Jarry Park. Much of that buzz centered on hot-hitting, red-haired outfielder Rusty Staub, or "*Le Grande Orange*," as he was lovingly nicknamed by Montreal's

French-speaking Expos supporters. And despite years of bad baseball played inside a tiny park, the Expos drew remarkably well.

That promised dome stadium arrived—at least partially—following the Summer Olympics in 1976. Olympic Stadium, or *Stade Olympique*, was a not-yet-domed dome on April 15, 1977, when the Expos moved in after years of delays, labor strife, and cost overruns. At $770 million, it was the most expensive stadium of its day. It was also one of the most maligned ballparks in the majors.

The elaborate stadium was built for Olympic events, not baseball. Its trademark is its 175-meter (about 575-foot) angled tower, which stands beyond center field and holds a Kevlar umbrella roof that is secured by 26 cables to allow movement. When the Expos arrived, there was no roof. There was, however, a track that was once paced by gold-medal winner Bruce Jenner and circled the artificial-turf field. Its capacity was over 60,000 thanks to three tiers of seats.

While far more modern than its predecessor, Olympic Stadium was seen by some as cold and unfriendly. And this feeling wasn't just because the roof was missing—fans were pushed far from the action by the sloped seating. Still, the young Expos attracted attention in the late 1970s by fielding exciting young talent like future Hall of Famers Gary Carter and Andre Dawson, and All-Star pitcher Steve Rogers. Crushing defeats kept the Expos at bay until 1981, when they made the playoffs for the first and only time. Poor management prompted the team to expend its talent pool; this, along with the team's inadequate ballpark, served to alienate its fans. A proposed new stadium—which was to be funded by the Expos, a beer company, and taxpayers—was unveiled in 2000; it never came to pass. In 2002, the team was sold to baseball's 29 other owners, and after the 2004 season, the Expos exited Montreal.

The American League also expanded north of the border—to Toronto, in 1977. The Blue Jays played their inaugural game there on April 7, just after a snowstorm hit the area. Their home, Exhibition Stadium, was a football field with an elbowed grandstand that masqueraded as a baseball park. Snow, seagulls, and anything else that blew off Lake Ontario would swirl overhead. In fact, one game in 1984 was postponed due to heavy winds.

In 1985, the Jays won their first division title, and they remained strong for years thereafter under the leadership of General Manager Pat Gillick. The harsh conditions Exhibition's tenants sometimes had to endure (especially during football season), however, convinced the government to finance a dome stadium. Exhibition was on its last legs. But, incredibly, more than two million fans passed through the stadium's gates in each of the Jays' final five full seasons there (1984–88).

Below: Before the Blue Jays arrived in 1977, Exhibition Stadium served as a setting for auto racing, concerts, circus shows, and Canadian Football League games, among other events. *Bottom: Stade Olympique* in Montreal was a showcase for the world during the 1976 Olympic Games. During Expos contests, though, it was often filled with more echoes than spectators.

NOT BIGGER IN ARLINGTON STADIUM

After seven seasons of hosting minor-league hopefuls, Arlington Stadium became the hottest spot—literally—in the big leagues. Daytime temps at the park frequently topped 100 degrees, prompting night games galore.

On Opening Day in 1972, a Texas-size jam of cars meandered its way toward the ballpark. Ahead of it was to be major-league baseball inside a not-so-major-league ballpark. Not long before, the road had led to Turnpike Stadium, home to the Dallas-Fort Worth Spurs of the Texas League. After the Washington Senators announced plans to relocate to Arlington for the 1972 season, officials tripled Turnpike's capacity to 35,000 and upgraded its name to major-league status.

To many, though, Arlington Stadium remained a minor-league ballpark for the 22 seasons the Texas Rangers called it home. "I enjoyed playing there," reliever Tom Henke told *Sports Illustrated*, "but it never gave you a big-league atmosphere."

Centrally located between Dallas and Fort Worth, Arlington Stadium rose from a bowl that sat 40 feet below ground level. For a time, this design allowed fans to enter at the top of the ballpark and walk down into a single-deck, uncovered grandstand. The outfield featured baseball's longest set of bleachers, a Texas-shape scoreboard, and heated air that either helped or hurt sluggers, depending on who was asked. On that first Opening Day, Rangers Manager Ted Williams signed autographs and posed with Little Leaguers. Despite the traffic jam outside, over 20,000 witnessed Frank Howard's monster home run in the Rangers' half of the first inning.

Early Rangers teams struggled while playing a plethora of night games due to the searing heat with which they would have had to contend during the day. The additional seats that were installed in the late 1970s (which pushed the park's capacity to over 41,000) were rarely needed; during some early seasons, the Rangers averaged fewer than 9,000 fans per game. However, on June 27, 1973, 18-year-old David Clyde—a former local high-school star—filled the house for his debut, a 4–3 win over the Twins. Few memorable nights would follow.

Respite for frustrated fans came in the ballpark's laid-back atmosphere— "Cotton-Eyed Joe" was played during the seventh-inning stretch, and it was where nachos made their big-league debut. Ageless Nolan Ryan infused the stadium with energy when he arrived in 1989; he would play the last five years of his illustrious career in a Rangers uniform. That same season, future President George W. Bush and his friends bought the Rangers. Thankfully, a real big-league park was on the horizon.

A remodeled Kauffman Stadium treated Royals fans to an improved game-day experience in 2009. Included in the upgrades were a children's playground and in-stadium miniature golf course.

ROYALS STADIUM GETS IT RIGHT

At a time when modern but bland concrete stadiums were used all around baseball, Royals Stadium was a *ballpark*. It hearkened back to days when one could recognize a city from outfield skyline of its ballpark.

While its contemporaries were overstated bowls, Royals Stadium was intimate—it offered seating for 40,625, a small number by standards of the time. The city, which built the park alongside Arrowhead Stadium, didn't skimp on details. This is one reason the park survives today while others of the era have met the wrecking ball.

"This stadium still has the charm of 1973 when it opened," Royals great George Brett said.

Royals Stadium is a baseball-only park—every seat is unobstructed and faces second base. There are no bleachers or multiple decks in the outfield; instead, there are waves of grass that serve as a landscape to a mesmerizing 322-foot waterfall display. A 12-story-high royally crowned scoreboard stands in center field alongside an 8,900-square-foot high-definition video board.

No ballpark is wart-free, however. Critics bemoan the stadium's remote location at a highway interchange, surrounded by parking lots and concrete. When it opened, it had artificial turf. (Grass was installed in 1995.) As a team, the Royals adapted well to their surroundings, parlaying speed and defense into a World Series championship in 1985 and six division titles in their first 13 seasons at Royals Stadium. The team consistently drew more than two million fans per season in baseball's smallest market from the late 1970s into the 1990s. Renamed Kauffman Stadium in 1993 in honor of long-time Royals owner Ewing Kauffman, the park underwent a $250-million renovation from 2007 to 2010 that will ensure its status as one of baseball's classics. It also hosted another World Series champion as the Royals were crowned in 2015.

HOK: BALLPARK RENAISSANCE

FANS CAN THANK three letters for the ballpark renaissance of the 1990s: HOK, the Babe Ruth of architects.

The sports division of the Kansas City–based firm of Hellmuth, Obata, and Kassabaum—better known as HOK Sport—ignited the "retro-classic" ballpark movement in 1991 with the new Comiskey Park. Oriole Park at Camden Yards, Jacobs Field, Coors Field, Comerica Park, Pacific Bell Park, and Enron Field followed soon after. The firm subsequently designed new stadiums in Pittsburgh, Cincinnati, Philadelphia, San Diego, St. Louis, Washington, and two in New York.

Each ballpark is unique, incorporating its neighborhood's landscape and history and making what was considered old new again. All over the world, for arenas, stadiums, and ballparks (both in the majors and minors), HOK was the go-to firm.

It all began in 1983 with a group of architects at HOK who envisioned a wealth of opportunities in sports facilities. They struck gold, eventually designing hundreds of sports stadiums and arenas around the globe.

THE MURPH IMPROVES WITH AGE

Sometimes, it's not how you start the race that counts most, but rather how you finish. That's good news for Jack Murphy Stadium, which charted an unusual course during its 35 years of hosting baseball in Mission Valley.

The Padres—born of the 1969 major-league expansion—played at San Diego Stadium. It was a multipurpose facility that had been financed by taxpayers at the urging of *San Diego Union* sports editor Jack Murphy, for whom the stadium would be renamed after his death in 1980.

Jack Murphy Stadium, "The Murph," wasn't a duplicate of the round concrete stadiums of the era. Surrounded by an expansive parking lot and the diverted San Diego River, it featured a U-shape grandstand that wrapped around left field. It offered an open view in right field, where bleachers and a scoreboard were stationed. Like most stadiums built in the 1960s, many of the park's 50,000 original seats were far from the Santa Ana Bermuda-grass playing field.

Thanks to Murphy's relentless persuasion, the San Diego Chargers—an American Football League power—arrived at the stadium in 1967. The expansion Padres followed two years later, losing 110 games while drawing less than 7,000 fans per contest in their first season. For the next 14 summers, the Padres continued to play like an expansion team and displayed their

marginal talent in heinous mustard-and-brown uniforms.

The Padres finished last in the NL West in each of their first six seasons. Attendance failed to top a million until 1974, and that milestone came amid rumors of relocation of the team to Washington, D.C. The Padres marked the occasion with a millionth-fan promotion late in the season—the team gave away cars and televisions.

Mayor Pete Wilson was moved to compliment team president Buzzie Bavasi on the club's drawing power. "He said it looked like we were vindicated for believing all along San Diego was a good baseball town," Bavasi said.

Ray Kroc, the McDonald's restaurant magnate, saved San Diego baseball when he bought the club in '74. Kroc convinced fans that he was committed to winning by taking the PA microphone during one particularly bad Padres performance to apologize directly for

"the stupidest ball-playing that I've ever seen in my life." Under Kroc, a famous San Diego performer made his debut: Ted Giannoulas, a 5'4", 125-pound college student, donned a pair of yellow tights and red feathers, transforming himself into the Famous Chicken, perhaps the most renowned mascot in sports. Losing, at least on occasion, became humorous.

An expansion of The Murph in 1982 saw the addition of 10,000 seats, which blocked the outfield view of a hillside;

Padres owner and McDonald's hamburger chain magnate Ray Kroc is greeted by perhaps the most famous mascot in sports, the Famous Chicken, during Kroc's 80th birthday celebration, held in 1982.

palm trees behind the outfield would have to suffice. But Kroc marched on—he spent his fast-food fortunes on veteran players in an effort to finally bring a winner to San Diego. Kroc died in January 1984 and never saw his dream realized. But with veteran recruits like Steve Garvey and Goose Gossage joining hometown hero Tony Gwynn, the Padres went to the World Series that fall (they lost to Detroit). Attendance soared, topping two million the following season. The Murph was expanded again in 1997 to accommodate the Chargers and the Super Bowl. The venue was renamed Qualcomm Stadium, as the telecommunications company paid $18 million to fund the completion of the renovation and thus received the naming rights. The Padres made a second World Series appearance in 1998, but lost in four games to the Yankees.

The Friars bade farewell to the facility after the 2003 season. A group of Marines carried its home plate to the team's new downtown home, Petco Park.

Left: Call it San Diego Stadium if you've been for around a while or Qualcomm if you're a youngster, but it was at "The Murph" that San Diego's Padres came of age. This pin from 1988 celebrates 20 years at the venue.
Below: After not finishing higher than fourth place in their previous 15 years of existence, the Padres gave fans a treat at "The Murph" in 1984 in the form of a surprising World Series appearance.

KINGDOME'S LIFE SHORT, NOT SWEET

At one time, the dome that stood along Seattle's Puget Sound housed the city's three major sports teams. And no stadium was louder when the home team was winning. But the Kingdome's life was short—and not particularly sweet.

The $67-million dome was Seattle's defense against the city's rainy weather and the bitterness that was felt after major-league baseball's one-season stop in the Pacific Northwest in 1969. The Seattle Pilots played one soggy summer at aging Sicks Stadium before their cash-strapped owners sold the club to Bud Selig, who transformed the team into the Milwaukee Brewers.

A lawsuit followed, as did construction of the Kingdome, which first welcomed the NFL's Seahawks in 1976. (The NBA's SuperSonics also played there for seven seasons beginning in 1978.) To settle the city's lawsuit over the Pilots' depar-ture, baseball granted Seattle an expansion team. The Mariners took to the Kingdome's artificial turf for the first time on April 6, 1977. Fourteen years later, they would have their first winning season.

The Kingdome was routinely criticized for its drab gray exterior and for its interior, which was not conducive to the game of baseball. It featured hanging speakers, one of which caught a foul ball hit by Mariner slugger Ruppert Jones in 1979. And when the Mariners weren't winning—which was often in the early days—the Kingdome, with its 60,000 mostly empty seats, was known as "The Tomb," due to its eerie gray quietness.

But The Tomb came to life in 1989 with the arrival of Ken Griffey Jr., who homered in his first at-bat at the Kingdome. The team improved, and by 1995, the Mariners were contenders. In addition to Griffey, the M's of the era also featured flamethrower Randy Johnson and batting champion Edgar Martinez. When it was filled to the ceiling, the Kingdome was ear-numbing; it was never more so than on October 8, 1995, when Griffey scored from first on a double by Martinez in the bottom of the 11th against the Yankees to give the franchise its first-ever postseason series win. This success led state legislators to approve funding for a new baseball-only facility. During the 1999 season, the Mariners moved to Safeco Field. The Kingdome was demolished in 2000; it has one of the shortest life spans of any modern stadium.

The unsightly Kingdome was oft-criticized during its short tenure as a big-league park, but Randy Johnson and Chris Bosio remember it as the site of their 1990 and 1993 no-hitters, respectively.

THE THUNDERDOME

During the 1987 World Series, Homer Hanky-waving Twins fans inside the Metrodome outroared a departing jet—their voices topped 120 decibels. Talk about home-field advantage!

The Hubert H. Humphrey Metrodome was as roundly disparaged as any indoor stadium. Its problems included its artificial surface, its white roof (in which fielders routinely lost balls), its overly cozy field dimensions, and its "Hefty Bag" wall in right field. But what endeared this dome to some was the play of the Twins, winners of thrilling seven-game World Series in 1987 and 1991, neither of which featured a Minnesota loss inside the "Thunder-dome." During 28 seasons under the dome's roof, in good times and bad, Twins fans came to expect the unexpected.

"I'm sure a couple of games were won because people lost a ball in the roof and stuff like that, but every ballpark has its own little quirks," former Twins first baseman Kent Hrbek told the *Saint Paul Pioneer Press*. "We lost ballgames because we stunk. We won because we were good."

Above right: Baseball's best players and young fans converged under the Metrodome roof in 1985 for the All-Star Game, as shown on the cover of this program. Though the park was known for homers, a record five bases were stolen in the NL's 6–1 victory. *Right:* Packed houses and high decibel levels were not unusual during the Metrodome's heyday, and it was that way in October 2009 when the facility hosted its last scheduled regular-season Twins game.

Officials broke ground on the Metrodome in 1979, with plans for it to serve as home to the Twins, the NFL's Vikings, and the University of Minnesota's football team. The Twins went indoors in 1982, leaving blustery Metropolitan Stadium behind; that year, the team's attendance almost doubled, to more than 920,000 (which was still last in baseball). While fans were warm, players were frustrated: In addition to defensive problems caused by the roof, pop flies sometimes struck speakers only to be caught for outs. The dome's air-pressure-supported roof required ten acres of fiberglass and 20 fans blowing hot air upward.

Seats used for football rolled back in right field, providing a short porch that sat 327 feet away. After many dingers were hit there, a 23-foot wall covered in a material that resembled a garbage bag was installed. In time, those championship Twin teams—which featured Hall of Famer Kirby Puckett and, in '91, hometown pitching great Jack Morris—made most forget the dome's shortcomings. After the 2009 season, the Twins left the Metrodome behind, moving outdoors again to Target Field.

Chapter 5

THE SECOND GOLDEN AGE

1989–Today

A building binge that started in the late 1980s brought on a second golden age for the shrines that house baseball. Real honest-to-goodness ballparks sprang up summer after summer. The first definitive masterpiece of the era was Baltimore's Oriole Park at Camden Yards, which inspired gems from Cleveland to San Francisco and from Texas to Minnesota.

Left: Even before the opening pitch was thrown at Camden Yards, the downtown Baltimore stadium earned acclaim as a game-changer with regard to the way fans would experience and enjoy a trip to the ballpark. *Above:* Souvenir baseballs—such as this 1990s model—fare better at Coors Field than actual game balls, which frequently get sent on long-distance rides through the thin Colorado air.

Rogers Centre, originally called "SkyDome," is a stadium and entertainment center in Toronto that opened in 1989 to host the Blue Jays and the Toronto Argonauts of the Canadian Football League; it cost more than $500 million to build. Under its retractable roof—and amid 348 hotel rooms, a Hard Rock Cafe, a 500-seat McDonald's, rows of luxury suites, a 300-foot bar, a miniature golf course, and $5 million worth of artwork—was a ballpark "like no other in the world."

"The new home of the Toronto Blue Jays and Toronto Argonauts is probably the future for a number of cities," writer Steve Wulf predicted at the new stadium's unveiling.

After all, SkyDome had *everything* under baseball's first-ever retractable roof. And despite failing to live up to its billing as the standard-bearer for future stadiums, SkyDome did blaze new trails—it was the first ballpark at which baseball seemed to be more of a sideshow in the face of so many other offerings. Contrary to Wulf's prediction, no carbon copies followed.

Since their inaugural season in 1977, the Blue Jays had endured playing home games at Exhibition Stadium. But in midseason 1989, the Jays moved to SkyDome. The facility's opening caused a media blitz, as reporters and fans alike gushed over what they found. It had taken seven years for the plans of architects Roderick Robbie and Michael Allen to come to fruition. Baseball had never before seen such a litany of amenities: restaurants, first-class shopping, 161 private skyboxes, and even a hotel with rooms overlooking the playing field.

SkyDome's most notable engineering achievement was 31 stories above the ground. The stadium's $100-million four-panel retractable roof can open or close in a mere 20 minutes. Made of steel and aluminum, it provides a sky view for the artificial-turf playing field and 90 percent of SkyDome's about 50,000 seats. The CN Tower rises beyond the right-field stands. Ironically, when the roof was retracted for the public during an extravagant opening ceremony, sheets of rain descended.

When the stadium was unveiled, the $17-million JumboTron scoreboard—33 feet high and 110 feet wide—was the world's largest. Toronto used SkyDome

Above: The holder of this ticket got to see the first World Series game ever held outside of the United States. The Blue Jays beat the Atlanta Braves in Game Three and eventually won the Series in six games. *Right:* The wonder of Rogers Centre is its retractable roof, a four-panel configuration that can be opened to blue skies or closed to the elements in a mere 20 minutes.

Right: Located just to the southwest of Toronto's most famous landmark, the CN Tower, Rogers Centre hosts not only the Blue Jays but also football, concerts, conventions, and more. *Bottom right:* Rogers Centre offers great views not only to those in the seats, but also to occupants of 70 rooms in the attached Renaissance Toronto Hotel, which overlook the playing field.

to support its claim as a world-class metropolis. "The eighth and ninth wonders of the world," Toronto Argonauts owner Harry Ornest said in 1989, referring to the CN Tower and SkyDome, respectively. "It is the most amazing and luxurious stadium I have ever been in, and I've been in all of them."

The Blue Jays produced amazing exploits at SkyDome almost immediately, winning World Series titles in 1992 and '93. The 1993 championship was won at SkyDome with Joe Carter's legendary ninth-inning walk-off home run. Fans responded—more than four million attended in 1991, '92, and '93, and the Blue Jays led the American League in attendance in each of the first six years of their residence at SkyDome.

In 1998, with the Blue Jays tumbling toward the bottom of the AL East and attendance sagging, SkyDome's ownership group went into bankruptcy. In 2000, Rogers Communications pur-

chased the team; then, in 2005, it bought the facility at the bargain basement price of $25 million—not much more than the original cost for the JumboTron alone—and renamed it "Rogers Centre." Several other clubs have since used the retractable-roof idea. But somehow, the extras that made SkyDome so intriguing more than 20 years ago now seem extraneous.

"Its vastness and greyness can give it the feel and sound of a mausoleum, the sterility of a hospital operating theatre," wrote *Toronto Star* columnist Garth Woolsey. "Its bells and whistles can't hide its oh-so-1989 feel."

NEW COMISKEY PARK SEEKS RENOVATED RESPECT

It may very well have been the Rodney Dangerfield of ballparks. The new Comiskey Park never got a whiff of respect—just an early facelift.

In 1991, it replaced the legendary field of the same name on Chicago's South Side. Wrigley Field, America's sweetheart of ballparks, sits across town. And in Baltimore, a retro-style ballpark that would revolutionize stadium design was rising as the new Comiskey was opening.

In some ways, the new Comiskey deserved the criticism. In other respects, it was inevitable.

After 80 seasons, there was no question that old Comiskey had to be replaced. White Sox owners Jerry Reinsdorf and Eddie Einhorn drove this point home by threatening to move their team to St. Petersburg, Florida. The Sox eventually got funding for their new stadium (which was built in the shadow of the original Comiskey) with a fixed government budget of about $167 million. The Illinois Sports Facility Authority, a quasi-public entity, built and ran the new park, the first baseball-only facility erected since Royals Stadium rose in 1973.

The planners at HOK Sport got some things right when they transferred features of the old Comiskey Park into the new stadium. The new Comiskey sports arched windows to reflect the old

An enduring symbol of the White Sox, the iconic scoreboard (along with some stands) from old Comiskey can be seen just beyond the new Comiskey's left-field upper deck.

Comiskey's outer facade, and the infield dirt was moved from the old park to the new one. What's more, the wild erupting scoreboard created by Bill Veeck for the old park was duplicated and enhanced.

On the downside, the upper deck was steep and far from the field, due in part to the approximately 90 luxury suites that circled the grandstand below. Fans also complained that other seats were further away than they had been at the old park. Ticket prices as well soared higher than a Frank Thomas home run, alienating the Sox's dogs-and-suds crowd. Despite this, attendance was strong the first several years there.

In 1992, just one year after the new Comiskey debuted, Oriole Park at Camden Yards opened to rave reviews. The comparisons between the two facilities were inevitable, and Comiskey did not fare well. HOK Sport designed both parks, and that's where the similarities ended. Less than ten years after the new Comiskey opened, the White Sox undertook a multiyear, multimillion-dollar series of renovations. All the seats were replaced, the scoreboard was revamped, restaurants and shops were opened, and a picnic area was added. The park's symmetrical outfield fences were tweaked. Statues honoring Carlton Fisk, Harold Baines, Nellie Fox, Luis Aparicio, Billy Pierce, Minnie Minoso, and Sox founder and longtime owner Charles Comiskey were installed. The eight uppermost rows of seats were removed and an amusement area was built as the ballpark's capacity settled at 40,000. The plastic surgery was partially funded by U.S. Cellular, which bought the stadium's naming rights—Comiskey Park became U.S. Cellular Field. In 2016, the stadium was again renamed Guaranteed Rate Field.

Much of the pain that Sox fans felt was alleviated in 2005, when the Pale Hose won their first World Series in 88 years. On the way to the Fall Classic, many of the criticisms of "The Cell" faded as South Siders embraced the team and its ballpark.

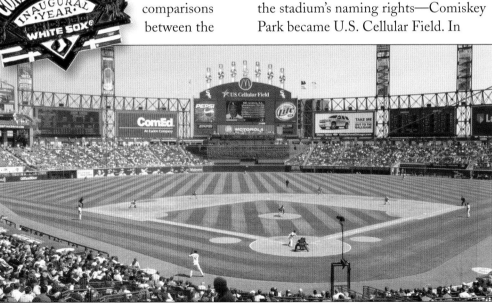

Above left: This glittering 1991 pin celebrates the sparkling new White Sox stadium, which stood within an off-speed pitch of the site of the old Comiskey Park. *Above:* Though the exploding scoreboard at Guaranteed Rate Field is actually larger than the one at the old Comiskey Park, it looks smaller to some in its larger surroundings.

PHILIP BESS AND ARMOUR FIELD

It was a field of dreams that never came to be. In the 1980s, Chicago architect Philip Bess designed a "neighborhood ballpark" that would have been built on the city's Armour Square Park, just north of Comiskey. Bess's idea would have preserved the old Comiskey playing field as a neighborhood park on 35th Street, and "Armour Field" would have relieved White Sox fans of the angst of the ballpark envy that came with their 1991 stadium.

Armour Field would have been quite different than new Comiskey. It was planned as an intimate and inviting ballpark, a real throwback to the 1910s, when diamonds were merged into neighborhoods. The plan called for a double-deck grandstand with shallow fences and natural sight lines that would open to a picturesque skyline beyond a wide-open outfield. A brick facade with dashes of windows would have been outside. Plans for surrounding residential and business structures were also included.

Bess's design never gained traction, but the ballpark remains alive today, if only on blueprints.

CAMDEN YARDS: MODERN MASTERPIECE

In 1992, Baltimore invited baseball fans to return to childhood, to a time when a ballpark anchored a neighborhood like an old friend. There it was: Oriole Park at Camden Yards.

Baltimore Orioles President Larry Lucchino had a vision for the team's new ballpark—how it should look, how it should feel. His disdain for the concrete slabs all around baseball was apparent. Lucchino was old-school; his team's ballpark would be as well. Baltimore, he knew, had just one chance to get it right. "We were not going to play in a ballpark we didn't want," Lucchino recalled.

Camden Yards was a game-changing concept. There would be so much more inside the gates than balls and strikes, than hits and runs. Lucchino, Orioles owner Eli Jacobs, chief architect Joseph Spear, O's Vice President Janet Marie Smith, and a battalion of engineering minds set out to create a great baseball experience that catered to fans while generating previously untapped revenue streams for ownership.

Unlike many of the super-stadiums of the 1960s and '70s, Camden Yards was cut into its downtown. It mixed perfectly into the historic landscape, much like Fenway Park does in Boston. "We just wanted to build a great little ballpark for Baltimore," Lucchino told *The Sun*. "We had no idea that the baseball world would embrace it."

Opening Day at Camden Yards was more than ten years in the making.

A short walk from Baltimore's Inner Harbor and a mere two blocks from the birthplace of Babe Ruth, Oriole Park at Camden Yards stands as one of baseball's most inviting modern venues.

Thoughts of a new ballpark for the O's began when Edward Bennett Williams bought the team in 1979. Ever since the franchise relocated from St. Louis, the team had played in cavernous Memorial Stadium. It was a large and impersonal facility that had been built for football—it was a gridiron, not a ballpark. Had a new venue been built at that time, officials would likely have sought a site along a pasture, near a highway, surrounded by vast parking lots, and between Baltimore and Washington, D.C., to best exploit the Beltway market (since Washington hadn't had a team since 1971).

This blueprint was tossed in the trash by Maryland Governor William Donald Schaefer, who saw the potential of an urban ballpark for Baltimore's Inner Harbor, just a long-toss from the birthplace of native son Babe Ruth. His idea promised to energize downtown Baltimore while reconnecting local fans to the game. Taxpayers would foot the $110-million tab, and politicians spoke of potential returns on their downtown-development investment.

The crux of design plans concerned the imposing and vacant Baltimore and Ohio Railroad warehouse—at more than 1,000 feet, it is thought to be the longest brick building on the East Coast. Despite his desire for an old-fashioned ballpark, Lucchino wanted the 19th-century eight-story behemoth brought down. Eric Moss, an architecture major at Syracuse University, however, envisioned incorporating the warehouse into a ballpark as part of his senior thesis. Moss showed his idea to the Baltimore

Planning Department, and they embraced the approach. Camden Yards' signature skyline vista beyond right field was created.

Oriole Park recalled the game's glory days, and ballparks built elsewhere would follow suit. When the venue opened on April 6, 1992, the entire baseball world was left breathless.

"It was really a jaw-dropping experience, from the clubhouse to the playing field, to the fans," said Orioles catcher Chris Hoiles, whose RBI double scored the ballpark's first run that afternoon. Instead of concrete, Camden Yards' outer facade is built of brick and iron, a throwback to Philadelphia's Shibe Park. Inside Oriole Park, visitors behind home plate can take in

Above right: This commemorative pin was issued to a lucky fan when Camden Yards hosted its first All-Star Game in 1993. The American League won the contest in a 9–3 romp. *Above:* Located on the former site of a railroad center, Oriole Park at Camden Yards—one of baseball's downtown gems—now welcomes fans who arrive by car, by bike, and on foot.

wide-open vistas of the stunning Baltimore skyline.

The B&O warehouse serves as a backdrop to Eutaw Street, a lively pedestrian walkway into Camden Yards that serves as a spot where fans can eat, drink, and converse. Inside the warehouse are three restaurants, a team merchandise shop, and assorted offices. A statue of a young Babe Ruth stands outside the gate, which leads to a pathway that's marked with brass baseball-shape plaques commemorating historic home runs. The walkway is surrounded by concessions—such as former slugger Boog Powell's barbecued delights—and tributes to Orioles greats and retired uniform numbers.

Three decks of unobstructed hunter-green seats engulf the playing field, bringing fans close to the action while creating an intimacy much like that of old Ebbets Field. Luxury suites and special seating cater to affluent fans. For added historic detail, the logo of the 1890s National League Orioles team is designed into every aisle seat. Like ballparks of the past, Camden Yards has an outfield that is asymmetrical, with a left-center-field wall that's farther away than center's, and the right-field fence a

mere 318 feet from home. A 25-foot wall with a small scoreboard that rises in right field adds another Ebbets-like feature to the ballpark. Ivy covers parts of a wall in center field that serves as the batter's eye, and advertising seems to blend in rather than blight the outfield views. A tiered bullpen lets everyone know which pitchers are warming up.

Orioles' fans flocked to their new treasure in droves—more than 3.5 million fans came out that first season. For years thereafter, Camden Yards

Below: Among the victorious American Leaguers who signed this ball from the 1993 All-Star Game at Camden Yards was MVP Kirby Puckett, who went 2-for-3 with a home run. *Right:* The shallow right-field fence fronting B&O Warehouse at Camden Yards is tempting for left-handed sluggers. During the 1993 Home Run Derby, Ken Griffey Jr. hit a ball off the warehouse.

In 2008, Oriole Park became the fastest stadium in baseball history to welcome its 50 millionth fan through its gates. It did so in a mere 17 years.

routinely sold out game after game, season after season. Other teams took notice. Retro, profit-generating downtown ballparks became all the rage. Never before had American sports witnessed a building explosion like the one ignited by Camden Yards.

The ballpark was the site of history in 1995, when Oriole great Cal Ripken Jr. eclipsed the once-thought unbreakable consecutive-games record of Lou Gehrig by playing in his 2,131st straight game.

The revenue generated by Camden Yards allowed the Orioles to acquire All-Star-quality players at most positions to complement Ripken, their homegrown hero. In 1997, the O's won the AL East while drawing 3.7 million spectators.

Few thought that the team had peaked, but as the years passed, the novelty of Camden Yards seemed to slowly wane. In 2008, the O's drew fewer than two million fans for the first time since the ballpark opened. Of course, much of this decline was due to the struggles of the Orioles at the time. They drew fewer than 10,000 fans to multiple games in 2010. However, the Orioles got back on the winning side of the ledger in 2012, bringing contending baseball back to a magical park that *Washington Post* writer William Gildea called, "traditional yet modern, considerate of baseball's past but cognizant of the the future."

JANET MARIE SMITH

JANET MARIE SMITH's fingerprints are all over Oriole Park at Camden Yards. She is often credited with making the Baltimore ballpark the most acclaimed of its era.

As the Orioles' vice-president of planning and development from 1989 to 1994, Smith was able to make sure that the park blended into its neighborhood. It was a plan that would be emulated by teams across baseball. Smith became one of the game's most sought-after talents. An architect and urban planner, Smith later had similar success in Atlanta, where she helped to turn an Olympic stadium into Turner Field. She later oversaw the expansion of Fenway Park in Boston.

She returned to Baltimore to help plan minor renovations as the park neared its 20th birthday, before taking a job as Senior VP of Planning and Development for the Dodgers in 2012. Her attention to detail remains intact, right down to the "Wee Willie" Keeler figures found on some of the ballpark's aisle seats. "We had a concept but had to turn it into details, and she was critical to that," said former Baltimore Orioles President Larry Lucchino.

Janet Marie Smith (right) talks with Boston Red Sox manager Terry Francona.

LIFE IN THE SUN

This brilliant ring is from the Marlins' World Series win in 1997. It was at Pro Player Stadium (now known as Sun Life Stadium) that the Florida Marlins won the Fall Classic in just the franchise's fifth season of play.

To the optimist, the legacy of Sun Life Stadium as a baseball venue is this: The Marlins won two World Series championships while calling it home. They defeated the Cleveland Indians in 1997 and the New York Yankees in 2003.

Beyond that, fans of the South Florida club will likely recall that Sun Life Stadium felt more like a gridiron than a baseball park. It's why there are no longer many multi-purpose stadiums hosting Major League baseball teams, and a large reason the Marlins and their supporters smiled their way to brand new Marlins Park in 2012.

Sun Life opened in 1987 as Joe Robbie Stadium, primarily for Robbie's Miami Dolphins of the NFL. It held 75,000 fans. During planning, provisions were made to enable a baseball diamond in the future; these modifications to the structure were made in the early 1990s. The National League expanded to Miami in 1993, thanks to owner Wayne Huizenga's dogged persistence. But despite its planners' forethought, the venue was always poorly configured for baseball. It was a football stadium. Its most notable baseball feature was the "Teal Monster," a 33-foot wall in left field that held the scoreboard.

When the Marlins arrived in Miami, they did so in a big way, winning a World Series in just their fifth season. But low attendance, paltry payrolls,

and groaning over the stadium threatened the franchise. Not even a second World Series title could turn things around. During the mid-2000s, Major League Baseball issued an ultimatum: Finance a new ballpark or risk losing the team.

The result was Marlins Park, and the end of Major League Baseball at Sun Life Stadium. The venue where the Marlins won two championships, where Ken Griffey Jr. socked his 600th career home run, and where Roy Halladay pitched the 20th perfect game in history is now back to doing what it does best— hosting football games played by the Miami Dolphins and the University of Miami Hurricanes.

Joe Robbie, Pro Player, Dolphin, Sun Life...the stadium in Miami has sported several names.

THE TROP LURES THE RAYS

St. Petersburg opened a stadium in 1990 to try to lure teams from Chicago, Seattle, and San Francisco. Unfortunately for residents, those cities opted to build new ballparks for their teams. Then, eight years after the stadium opened, major-league baseball splashed down in St. Pete when the expansion Tampa Bay Devil Rays arrived, in 1998.

Since renamed Tropicana Field ("The Trop"), the tilted-roof dome has been derided. It was built for $138 million—with a renovation in 1996 that cost another $85 million. The 43,000-seat stadium features a five-story rotunda modeled from blueprints that were used to create the grand entrance of Ebbets Field, which leads fans through a 900-foot mosaic walkway made of more than 1.8 million tiny ceramic tiles. The outfield fences are artificially asymmetrical. FieldTurf, a realistic artificial grass, allows The Trop to present all-dirt basepaths.

The dome features the world's second-largest cable-supported roof, which is made of translucent fiberglass. Over second base, the ceiling rises to 225 feet; above center field, it dips to 85 feet. The four catwalks that hang above the diamond have been known to confound outfielders. The dome's lid is tilted for better cooling and hurricane protection, and it is illuminated in orange after Rays victories.

The Trop offers many amenities, including tanks with more than 30 live rays that sit just beyond right-center field, near a children's play area. "Center

Tropicana Field—with its tilted roof and unusual catwalks—has hosted Rays games and sparse crowds since the team's inception. It finally witnessed success when the club won 2008 American League pennant.

Field Street" features a bar and restaurant from which to view games. The Ted Williams Museum and Hitters Hall of Fame was relocated to beyond center field in 2006 after its original location in Hernando, Florida, closed.

Lousy Rays teams have not helped attendance at The Trop. In their first ten seasons, the Rays lost many more games than they won. In 2008, however, their fortunes changed as they battled their way into the World Series. The team has gone back and forth over the past several years in trying to decide on a location and feasible plan for a much-needed new ballpark.

THE JAKE BRINGS COLOR TO CLEVELAND

Terrific sight lines, comfortable seats, a wide variety of food and beverages, and kids' activities are among the many modern amenities available to fans during Indians' games.

Remember when Dorothy opened her door and crept into the colorful Land of Oz? That movie scene was repeated, sans Toto, when the Cleveland Indians marched into Jacobs Field. Although just blocks from their shopworn black-and-white lakefront digs at Municipal Stadium, Jacobs Field—"The Jake"— seemed to be a million miles away in terms of ambiance.

For more than 60 years (on and off), the Tribe toiled in the cavernous, dark, and often vacant Municipal Stadium. But at the corner of Carnegie and Ontario, The Jake ushered in a whole new era for Indian fans. When the ballpark's iron gates swung open in April 1994, a team—and, indeed, an entire city—turned a corner. "It marked the day Cleveland once again adopted the

Indians as its own after a four-decade renunciation," Jonathan Knight wrote in his book, *Opening Day*.

Indians owner Richard Jacobs set the wheels in motion in the late 1980s, when he collaborated with city and county leaders to correct the so-called "Mistake by the Lake" (as Municipal Stadium was called). Jacobs paid about $10 million for the naming rights, and he was able to

convince voters to approve a funding proposal in which higher alcohol and cigarette taxes paid for construction. The Jake's price tag was set at $175 million; a neighboring arena, now called Quicken Loans Arena, ran another $150 million.

While Jacobs handled the business end of the franchise, general manager John Hart crafted the Indians' fortunes on the field. Through shrewd trades and drafting, Hart laid the foundation for a spectacular Indians' lineup, the likes of which Cleveland hadn't seen in more than four decades. The city had not witnessed a championship since the Browns won the 1964 NFL title; the Indians had not come close to sniffing a pennant since 1959.

Cleveland needed Jacobs Field as much as the Indians did. The city was down on its luck, abiding in the shadow of financial collapse. The ballpark and the adjoining arena served as the center-pieces of a downtown revitalization project. Jacobs Field was the second facility built as part of baseball's "retro-classic" park movement, a trend that was to be followed by half of the major leagues' 30 teams. Its design followed the classic style of Camden Yards while integrating Cleveland's rich industrial history. A brick and exposed-iron exterior corresponds with its neighbors in the south-downtown landscape.

Inside, The Jake is everything Municipal Stadium wasn't. Looking out from home plate, one can take in a stellar view of the Cleveland skyline. Open-air concourses allow fans to walk around the lower deck, seeking choice concessions while still taking in the action. A glass-

enclosed restaurant overlooks left field. Tiers of luxury suites—including a set on the field behind home plate—cater to the city's elite.

The venue's 35,225 seats—reduced from a max capacity of 41,000—point to the infield and cover two decks with mezzanines in right field and along the first-base line. Details didn't evade the

park's designers: Ornate iron carvings adorn aisle seats, and cup holders are within easy reach. The upper deck, although steep and distant, offers dramatic views of the city, both from the seating bowl and the terrace concourse. Nineteen light standards that are shaped like giant toothbrushes offer distinctive brightness.

Its urban setting and magnificent architecture made the home of the Indians a smashing success in Cleveland and beyond when Jacobs Field opened its doors in 1994.

REVITALIZATION AT THE JAKE

THE UNVEILING OF Jacobs Field in 1994 launched the revitalization of a baseball franchise and a city. Cleveland was transformed from a place that players dreaded into a playground for the game's very best. During this renaissance, free agents actually wanted to come to the North Coast, and for good reason: Never before had the Indians dominated its American League competition for such an extended period.

In 1995, the Indians finished first in the AL Central, ending a 41-year title drought in record-setting fashion by capturing the division by a whopping 30-game margin. Five more division titles and two World Series appearances followed through 2001. During this stretch, the Indians sent six players to the All-Star Game three different times. Tribe players won 11 Silver Slugger awards and 14 Gold Gloves from 1995 to 2001.

In 1997, Jacobs Field became one of the few ballparks to host the All-Star Game and the World Series in the same year. From 1995 to 2001, it sold out for 455 consecutive games, pushing attendance beyond the three million mark each year from 1996 to 2001.

This ticket got a fan into Jacobs Field's first game in 1994.

Stadium workers blow snow off the field on Opening Day 2007 in Cleveland, where northern Ohio temperatures and Lake Erie winds can still play havoc on Indians games.

The grass is Kentucky bluegrass, not painted dirt like at the old stadium after a Browns game. In The Jake's outfield, an asymmetrical fence juts in and out. A miniature version of Boston's Green Monster rises 19 feet in left field; atop it is a plaza where fans can stand along an iron railing. A set of 2,700 bleacher seats is situated next to the plaza, anchoring a massive 120-foot-tall scoreboard that has a script "Indians" mounted at its top. In a concourse beyond center field sits a statue of the greatest Indians pitcher ever, Bob Feller.

On Opening Day 1994, the Indians featured former and future All-Stars at nearly every position. The team found itself in a pennant race. That summer's labor dispute dashed the hopes of Cleveland fans, however, as the season was cut short in August with the Indians a game out of first place. In 1995, the Tribe rushed out of the gate, dominating American League foes. Jacobs Field, meanwhile, began a sell-out streak on June 12. It would last for a baseball-record 455 consecutive regular-season games, until April 4, 2001. Often during this stretch, all three million tickets were sold before the first game; sometimes they were gone before Christmas. Those without tickets paid a nominal fee just to tour the park. The Tribe was that good.

"A new ballpark, an All-Star cast, and the end of a long history of losing all came together to inspire fans," wrote

Cleveland columnist Terry Pluto in his book, *Dealing*.

The World Series came to town in the fall of 1995, after the city celebrated its first AL pennant in more than four decades. The loss to Atlanta in that Fall Classic only whetted the city's appetite for a championship. A string of division titles followed, as did another trip to the Series in 1997. That year, in typical hard-luck Cleveland fashion, the Tribe blew a ninth-inning lead in Game 7 and fell to the Marlins. Successful seasons followed, but none matched the magic of the 1990s.

Richard Jacobs—who, along with his brother, David, bought the Indians for about $40 million in 1986—had exhausted the club's profit potential by 2000. That year, he sold the club to the Dolan family for $323 million. Larry Dolan said that Richard Jacobs achieved success in Cleveland baseball unmatched "since Bill Veeck in the '40s."

Over the years, The Jake has undergone subtle changes while the team has endured major renovations. Progressive Insurance purchased the stadium's naming rights in 2008, after Jacobs' agreement had expired. The Indians, meanwhile, have undergone several periods of rebuilding, including one that resulted in another AL pennant in 2016. The ballpark hosted one of the most memorable Game 7s in World Series history that year. Unfortunately for Clevelanders, their Indians fell short against the Chicago Cubs in a 10-inning classic. The ballpark, however, remains far more than a victory for the city and its long-suffering fans. It's truly a crown jewel.

Above: Just one year after making then-Jacobs Field their home in 1994, the Indians welcomed their fans to the first of five straight seasons of playoff appearances, including two World Series berths. *Left:* Though a naming-rights purchase by Progressive Insurance brought down the "Jacobs Field" sign in January 2008, the home of the Cleveland Indians remains "The Jake" to local fans.

THE BALLPARK IN ARLINGTON BLENDS INGREDIENTS

The Ballpark in Arlington (renamed Globe Life Park in Arlington in 2014) emerged from a blender that contained a spoonful of Tiger Stadium, a dash of Wrigley, a pinch of Fenway, and a smidgen of Ebbets. Despite this, the Rangers' home still offers its own distinct flavor and is a worthy entrant in the "retro-classic" ballpark era. But its birth was not without controversy.

There was little question of need. Arlington Stadium, the team's home since 1972, was a venue that hardly befit major-league baseball. The issue of financing a new ballpark fell to taxpayers, and the club's owners threatened relocation if funding wasn't approved. George W. Bush, son of then-President George H. W. Bush, bought a small stake in the Rangers in 1989 and served as the team's face before stepping down to run for governor of Texas in 1994. With his family's influence, Bush got what he wanted: public money to build his team's new $190 million home. The stadium took just 23 months to finish.

Architects planned a ballpark that borrowed from other parks. The outer red-brick-and-granite archways recall Comiskey Park. In right field, a roofed double-deck grandstand—which resembles Tiger Stadium's fabled home run porch, columns and all—provides a tantalizing tater target. The center-field bleachers evoke memories of Wrigley Field. The foul poles and some bleachers were transplanted from Arlington Stadium. A grassy knoll beyond center appears to have been influenced by Kansas City's Kauffman Stadium. A manual scoreboard embedded inside a 14-foot wall in left reminds some of Fenway Park. And although its shape is not necessitated by the restrictions of its surroundings, the asymmetrical outfield wall has eight different angles that produce wacky bounces and caroms like those encountered at Ebbets Field.

Regardless of its influences, this park is still all about Texas. Sitting on a 270-acre site about a quarter-mile from the old stadium, the park features an imposing brick exterior made from "Sunset Red" granite mined from nearby Marble Falls. Thirty-five stone longhorns and 21 Lone Stars affixed to the brick give visitors that Texas feel.

Inside, shallow fences and seats that face home plate offer an intimacy to

The Ballpark in Arlington is the popular centerpiece of a 270-acre entertainment complex that also includes a 12-acre lake, parks, and outdoor recreation space on the perimeter.

fans—49,115 of them when the park is filled. Borrowing another classic trait, the venue features a section of right-field-corner seats that allows spectators to see the game through a fence opening. A steel canopy adorns the roof. The stadium offers five levels of seating, including 120 luxury suites and Lexus Club seats. Four stories of team offices stand beyond the center-field wall.

Once on the Bermuda Tifway surface, players immediately noted the park's propensity to play as a hitter's paradise. From home plate, it is 332 feet to the left-field foul pole, 400 feet to straightaway center, 381 feet to the right-center power alley, and a scant 325 feet to the right-field pole.

These distances may have pleased homer-happy Rangers fans—attendance records were smashed—but pitchers saw their ERAs balloon. The Rangers' staff went from sixth to 13th in the league in ERA in 1994, immediately after the move. Nevertheless, success in the standings followed, as the Rangers won their division for the first time in 1996, ending a 35-summer dry spell. Division titles followed in 1998 and '99, but those postseason runs ended with spankings from the Yankees, as the Rangers managed just one victory in three Division Series playoffs. 2010 and '11 saw back-to-back trips to the World Series.

Under the lead of an ownership group that includes Hall of Famer and former Rangers ace Nolan Ryan since the former management group declared bankruptcy in 2010, Texas added two more division titles in 2015 and '16 while continuing to draw great crowds.

Top: When it comes to net worth, forget the face-value prices on these uncut tickets to The Ballpark's 1994 debut now that Hall of Famer Nolan Ryan has signed them. *Right:* By attracting well over two million fans per season, the Arlington facility helped the Rangers finish third in AL attendance in two of the park's first three years.

COORS FIELD: ROCKY MOUNTAIN HIGH

Pitchers have come to embrace the one area of Coors Field where it's always a pleasant 70 degrees: the humidor. Hurlers can thank the boots of Tony Cowell for this nerve-calming, ERA-saving space. We all know why Denver is called the Mile High City, and we've learned what thin air in high altitude does (or doesn't do) to a flying baseball—it's a hitter's heaven, a pitcher's pain.

It took just three innings before the first home run sailed out of Coors Field after it opened in 1995. The dingers didn't stop. One season, teams combined to average 15 runs a game there while knocking 303 four-baggers in 81 games. Ordinary hitters became Ruthian while pitchers ducked for cover.

Enter Cowell, a Rockies engineer, who happened to notice the effect that Denver's low humidity had on his leather hunting boots, which had become tight and dry. If the air affected his boots, he thought, imagine what it must do to baseballs. Pitchers at Coors also complained of balls that were cold and difficult to grip. With this in mind, major-league baseball's first humidor was

Above: National League offense got a jolt—and pitchers an unwanted wake-up call—when Coors Field opened its high-altitude gates in 1995, as this pennant commemorates. *Right:* "The Player," a nine-and-a-half-foot statue that honors baseball pioneer Branch Rickey, was unveiled in front of the classic main entrance to Coors Field in 2005.

installed in 2002 at Coors Field. The climate-controlled shed with 50 percent humidity can store 576 baseballs and is considered a Colorado-bound pitcher's best friend.

An expansion team that began play in 1993, the Colorado Rockies played their first two seasons at Mile High Stadium, which they shared with the NFL's Broncos. The Rockies' attendance was mind-boggling—nearly 4.5 million came out that first season. As a result, planners of Coors Field expanded seating by more than six thousand before it opened, giving the ballpark room for more than 50,000 fans.

Coors opened on April 26, 1995, in the city's historic downtown "LoDo" neighborhood, which is filled with 19th-century brick structures. The ballpark fit right in. Its facade is comprised of both terra-cotta tile and exposed steel and red brick. The stadium is topped by a classic clock tower, but it also bears amenities typical of the modern era, including more than 4,500 club-level seats, 63 luxury suites, a restaurant and brewery, a children's play area, and

batting cages. Seats along the first-base line offer spectacular views of the Rocky Mountains. Water fountains beyond the outfield fence erupt after home runs. "The Rockpile," a set of 2,300 bleacher seats, is perched above the center-field backdrop. And to remind everyone of the thin air, a row of purple seats extends around the upper deck to mark the exact point at which the park is one mile above sea level.

In their first year at Coors, the Rockies qualified for the playoffs for the first time. In 2007, five years after the humidor began softening baseballs, the Rockies battled into the World Series. Debate lingers over how much credit should be afforded Cowell's boots.

MILE HIGH PACKS 'EM IN

COORS FIELD, FOR all its retro style, can never top Mile High Stadium, the Rockies' original home—at least when it comes to attendance.

Originally called Bears Stadium, the park sat 17,000 people when it opened in 1948. It was home to Denver's minor-league team, but reaching the majors was the city's ultimate goal. By the time the Rockies were born in 1993, the facility had already been greatly expanded and renamed Mile High Stadium. At the time, it served as the home of the NFL's Broncos.

While Coors Field was being built, the Rockies made Mile High their home. Converting the football stadium into a baseball park meant that the entire east grandstand had to be moved along hydraulic tracks. Ever so gently, it was shifted 145 feet in two hours. On Opening Day 1993, a record 80,227 were on hand to witness the first game in Rockies history. By season's end, nearly 4.5 million spectators had visited. Since many of today's ballparks are roughly half the size of Mile High, these records will likely remain untouched for the foreseeable future.

The jewel of the "LoDo" neighborhood in downtown Denver, Coors Field features a landmark entry arch adorned with distinctive panels that pay tribute to various types of balls.

PHOENIX RISING: CHASE FIELD

Chase Field in Phoenix is the only ballpark in which lounging fans can shout for operators to close the roof from a swimming pool; where water canons erupt for home runs; where grass grows under a ceiling; and where baseballs, footballs, and basketballs have been hit, kicked, and shot. At the Arizona Diamondbacks' home, amenities—some might call them distractions—are plentiful: the retractable roof that moves to its own musical tune, a blinding 136-foot-wide scoreboard, and a swimming pool that sits behind the wall in right-center, 415 feet from home plate.

Originally named Bank One Ballpark, or "The BOB," when it first opened, the stadium boasts modern conveniences and engineering feats while simultaneously attempting to reach back into baseball's rich history. Its $354-million price tag (which was footed by taxpayers), however, was ultramodern. Diamondback fans nevertheless embraced the ballpark (which seats over 48,000) and the expansion team when they debuted in 1998. More than one million fans passed through the turnstiles in the stadium's first 22 games. The

facility hosted more than three million attendees in both of the franchise's first two seasons.

Like many of the "retro-classic" stadiums, Chase Field was incorporated into its downtown neighborhood. With its red brick and exposed steel, the

GIFT CERTIFICATE

The Bearer of this gift certificate is entitled to the unique experience of opening the roof at Bank One Ballpark prior to a 2005 regular season Arizona Diamondbacks home game.*

Above right: For all the excitement a baseball game can bring, being able to open the roof of the Bank One Ballpark—as the lucky holder of this certificate was able to do—must be an event unto itself. *Above:* The designers of Chase Field incorporated concepts from the downtown Phoenix warehouse district into their plans, and even used a real warehouse to form part of the facility's south facade.

Chase Field's air-conditioning system is designed to lower the temperature by 30 degrees in three hours. It is welcome relief to those not watching from the stadium's famed swimming pool, located in right-center field.

building fits nicely into the city's historic warehouse district. In fact, the former Arizona Citrus Growers' Packing House is kept in partial use as the ballpark's concession-stand commissary. Colorful murals decorate the exterior. Inside, natural grass grows around a dirt pitcher's path between home plate and the mound, and the outfield features a mostly symmetrical fence.

No ballpark built under the blazing Arizona sun would be complete without a roof and air conditioning, both of which Chase Field offers. The nine-million-pound steel roof opens and closes to the sound of music that is timed to accompany the four-and-a-half minute move. The roof remains open

during the day to help the grass grow, and the weather dictates whether it remains open or is shut for a game. The ballpark's air-conditioning unit can cool the building in a matter of three hours. This versatility has allowed the park to be used for football, soccer, and basketball, in addition to baseball.

The D-backs found success in Chase Field almost immediately, winning their division in just their second season of play. A World Series title followed in 2001, a year in which the D-backs boasted pitching aces Curt Schilling and Randy Johnson. Arizona became the first team in Series history to rally from a ninth-inning deficit in Game 7 to win the crown without needing extra innings.

GROUND-POOL DOUBLE

IT IS THE only ballpark in which fans can relax in a hot tub and a batter can hit a "ground-pool double." Yes, Chase Field in Phoenix offers more than just baseball, peanuts, and hot dogs.

The RideNow Powersports swimming pool sits beyond the park's right-center-field fence. It has room for up to 35 fans to take a refreshing swim for a not-so-refreshing $5,500 a game. A home run hit by Mark Grace of the Cubs was the first to reach the water on the fly on May 12, 1998. On April 3 of that year, however, Diamondback third baseman Matt Williams hit the first "ground-pool double" when his batted ball bounced over the fence and into the three-foot-deep water.

While the pool gets the majority of the attention, there are other noteworthy diversions at Chase, such as the Peter Piper Playhouse for kids and the Cox Clubhouse, which features memorabilia from the National Baseball Hall of Fame.

Fans watch Game 1 of the 2001 World Series from the pool at Bank One Ballpark.

SEATTLE'S BEST: SAFECO FIELD

Going from the tomblike grayness of the Kingdome to the brilliant greenness of Safeco Field was Seattle's journey to baseball nirvana.

Safeco offers fresh Puget Sound air, which circles the sparkling ballpark. It features sun-cast shadows over real grass, the city skyline in the distance, and the whistling of passing trains. "A day this good, in a stadium this lush, makes baseball feel like a newly discovered form of theology," wrote *Seattle Times* columnist Steve Kelley. "This is almost heaven."

Mariner fans found happiness at Safeco Field, another installment in baseball's "retro-classic" stadium frenzy. The ballpark began its existence as the object of financing controversy, as Washington politicians approved a tax plan to fund its construction almost immediately after voters rejected a similar proposal. Regardless, the $517-million ballpark opened in 1999 in midseason to sellout crowds—tickets were scalped for hundreds of dollars over their face values. Safeco is named for the Seattle-based insurance company that paid over $35 million for the rights.

The stadium was praised by ballpark aficionados as much for its brick-laden exterior as for the innovation, artwork, and attention to detail that lie inside. The main rotunda, circular and stately, is reminiscent of parks gone by and fits into Seattle's "SoDo" downtown district. The exterior's more than 600,000 bricks surround glass windows and exposed steel.

Inside, Safeco is the anti-Kingdome. Its field is composed of blended grass, modern seating is available for more than 47,000 baseball fans over four decks, and a traditional hand-operated scoreboard tracks balls and strikes. The park also has loads of amenities, museums, and play areas. It's most unique element, however, is up above.

To beat back the cold and rain that is notorious in the Pacific

Sunsets over Puget Sound, an occasional view of Mount Rainier, and state-of-the-art amenities distinguish Safeco Field among baseball's most stunning recently built venues in which to experience a game.

Northwest, Safeco Field was built with a telescoping retractable roof that acts like an umbrella—shielding but not enclosing the playing field. The roof covers nine acres, and the Mariners claim that it contains enough steel to build a 55-story skyscraper. When the roof is retracted, it sits over the tracks of the nearby BNSF Railway, one of four remaining transcontinental rail lines. The park's proximity to the tracks offers sights and sounds of days when trains connected America's coastlines. On occasion, Mount Rainier can be seen in the distance.

"The roof at climate-controlled Bank One Ballpark in Phoenix acts like a sunroof on a luxury car," wrote Seattle scribe Blaine Newnham. "Safeco Field's roof will fall back more like a ragtop on an old VW."

In the team's first 18 seasons—1977 to 1994—the M's never finished higher than third in their division. All that changed in 1995, as superstar sluggers Ken Griffey Jr. and Edgar Martinez, along with frightening southpaw hurler Randy Johnson, led the way to a first-place finish at the Kingdome. Success followed the M's to Safeco. In 2001, the team won a record-tying 116 games. Yet that year, for the third time in seven seasons, the M's lost the AL Championship Series. At the gate, however, the Mariners were champions, drawing more than three million fans each year from 2001 to 2003.

Safeco Field fans witnessed 116 regular-season wins in 2001. The Mariners led the American League in attendance in the 2001 and 2002 seasons.

SAFECO SHOWCASES LOCAL ART

A CHANDELIER SCULPTURE called *The Tempest* hangs above the ornate main concourse rotunda, and it tells all that Safeco Field is not just a palace for athletes—it's also a showcase for artists.

The chandelier, which is composed of more than a thousand translucent baseball bats illuminated with incandescent lights, is just one of dozens of pieces of artwork on display throughout the ballpark. The collection includes paintings, prints, and photographs from Seattle-area artists.

The most notable piece at Safeco is a six-foot-tall sculpture of an umpire making a safe call. The work by Scott Fife portrays Emmett Ashford, the first African American umpire in the Pacific Coast League. Other popular pieces include Ross Palmer Beecher's metal quilts, two of which are made from discarded materials and stitched to state and Canadian province license plates to recreate the logos of baseball's 30 franchises.

The display of this artwork was planned from Safeco's inception: Original ballpark plans called for $1.3 million to be spent on the works.

Artist Donald Fels—from nearby Fall City, Washington—crafted metal sculptures of six basic pitches; they hang on the parking garage columns outside Safeco Field.

MINUTE MAID TO ORDER IN HOUSTON

Twenty-four-dollar box-seat tickets for an Astros' *preseason* game in 2000 against the defending-champion New York Yankees sold for more than $400. This record-setting rush was for a first glimpse of Houston's new ballpark. And although Houstonians would like to forget its original name—"Enron Field"—the downtown ballpark, with all its gadgets and gizmos, endures as a hitter's paradise in an era in which runs matter more than strikeouts or shutouts. The city that gave baseball the Astrodome offers its

retractable-roof facility as another model for others to emulate.

"Just as Houston paved the way for domed stadiums," Mayor Lee Brown said, "we're paving the way right now for a new era of stadiums in this country, if not the world."

There's no mistaking Houston's ballpark, with its brick-and-limestone facade set in a rich, historic neighborhood. When it opened, it bore the name of energy giant Enron, but scandal at the company led the Astros to buy out the

$100-million 30-year contract after two seasons and resell the naming rights to Coca-Cola. Shortly thereafter, the soft-drink company slapped its Minute Maid brand all over the ballpark.

Located at the corner of Crawford and Texas streets in downtown Houston, Minute Maid Park was built at a cost of nearly $250 million. Many fans attending games at Minute Maid pass through Union Station, the city's recently renovated century-old train depot, where the Astros' team store and a café are housed.

It takes between 12 and 20 minutes for the 242-foot-high roof to open and close at Minute Maid Park. That's faster than many pitchers can record three outs in this hitter's haven.

Like parks of the past, this 41,676-seat stadium was squeezed into its neighborhood, giving it a short home-run porch in left field that sits just 315 feet from home. It is so close to the plate that special dispensation was needed from Major League Baseball to allow it. Its 21-foot wall—which features a scoreboard below the 763 seats in the "Crawford Boxes"—makes hitters drool and pitchers pray. An old-fashioned gasoline pump on the "Conoco Home Run Porch" keeps a running tally of Astro dingers that pass by.

"I don't know whose idea the left-field line was. He's not my friend," Astros pitcher Jose Lima told reporters as he took in his new ballpark home in 2000. Lima went from being a 20-game winner in 1999 while at the Astrodome to a 16-game loser who surrendered an NL-record 48 home runs in his first season at Enron Field.

Serving as a backdrop—and as a tribute to the city's railroad history—is an arched cream-color wall that stretches approximately 800 feet from left field to center. Above the wall, a replica locomotive chugs after Astro home runs. Pitchers find solace in center field where the fence sits 435 feet from home, and beyond "Tal's Hill," a slope that pays homage to "Duffy's Cliff" at Boston's Fenway Park and the "terrace" at Cincinnati's Crosley Field. As if this rise wasn't quirky enough, a flagpole stands in fair territory atop the slope, an idiosyncrasy that was borrowed from old Tiger Stadium. The hill was named after Astros president Tal Smith, but he steadfastly denies that he had any part in its design, which sometimes produces embarrassment for stumbling outfielders.

In right field are a double-deck grandstand, a state-of-the-art scoreboard, and a popular four-level patio. The ballpark's retractable roof, which helps make baseball in Houston bearable, sits above the right-field stands when open. When the roof is retracted, Minute Maid Park has the largest open area of any ballpark with a movable roof in baseball.

After a rocky start at their new park, the Astros quickly grew accustomed to Minute Maid, making the playoffs three times in their first six years there. A Houston-record three million fans visited the stadium in 2000, its first season. In 2005, the Astros made their first appearance in the World Series, which they lost to the Chicago White Sox. In 2017, they returned, this time with a different outcome. beating the Dodgers in the deciding seventh game.

A 50,000-pound 1860s-replica train, built by the same company that provided the retractable roof's transporters, chugs along the 800 feet of track above Minute Maid Park's left-field fence.

An ultramodern retractable roof and a 1911 railroad stop (Union Station) that serves as an entrance highlight the blend of past and present that is Minute Maid Park.

SPLASH HIT: SAN FRANCISCO'S AT&T PARK

Of all the ballparks to emerge in the "retro-classic" era, AT&T Park—with its iconic location along the San Francisco Bay—may be the grandest of them all. Its setting's natural beauty is unsurpassed, its views unparalleled, and its quirkiness unpredictable. Even the advertising inside the ballpark draws aesthetic praise.

The stadium features tributes to the Giants' rich tradition, including a nine-foot statue of Willie Mays at the entrance. A children's playground, a giant baseball-glove sculpture, and a miniature version of the ballpark behind left field are popular attractions.

Still, much of AT&T Park's allure to ballpark enthusiasts lies beyond right field in the inviting waters of McCovey Cove, where boaters tailgate and mammoth home runs plop. Perhaps no ballpark fits its hometown better.

Critics and historians routinely place AT&T Park atop lists of baseball's brightest and most fan-friendly ballparks. Credit for its design and its adherence to baseball tradition falls to Giants owner Peter Magowan, who saved San Francisco baseball in the early 1990s and delivered AT&T Park in 2000. Giants fans escaped the dark, gloomy confines of Candlestick Park for a waterfront palace. Gone, for the most part at least, are the cold, gusty winds that marred old Candlestick. In an age in which taxpayer dollars are routinely used to build new stadiums, Magowan secured financing that covered much of AT&T Park's $357-million price tag and led a season-ticket-marketing campaign that helped the ballpark become the first privately funded baseball-only facility constructed since Dodger Stadium was completed in 1962.

Originally named Pacific Bell Park, AT&T Park fit Magowan's vision of a classic baseball facility, which was inspired by Fenway Park and Wrigley Field. Architects followed the designs of newer parks in Baltimore, Cleveland, and Denver to draw its marvelous blueprint. Every view that causes a diehard to stare, every outfield nook that causes a baseball to ricochet, and every amenity that causes a patron to celebrate was calculated and measured with the fan in mind. Magowan, an aficionado of the game himself, made sure of it.

"For a fan, it may be the best park ever built," said baseball writer Peter Gammons. "But then, it takes a fan to understand one."

AT&T Park sits in a once-desolate warehouse section of San Francisco, sandwiched between the bay and the downtown skyline. Whether patrons

With the San Francisco skyline on one side and boats and kayaks dotting China Basin (also known as McCovey Cove) on the other, AT&T Park is perfectly situated for Giants fans.

travel by foot, bike, car, subway, ferry, or one of San Francisco's famed streetcars, no other ballpark offers such easy access, which is shown by the three million fans the Giants attracted during each of the first eight seasons they played at their new home.

Every game at the ballpark takes on a carnivallike summer atmosphere. Fans congregate in a waterfront promenade along the bay. Boats, kayaks, canoes, and surfboards—numbering in the dozens and often equipped with radios or TVs—await well-struck baseballs from inside the stadium. China Basin, where the

watercraft gather, has become known as McCovey Cove, in tribute to famed Giants' slugger Willie McCovey.

Inside, AT&T Park has one of baseball's most unique playing fields, from its naturally blended grass to its jagged outfield fence, which drives outfielders batty. Its nearest wall sits 309 feet from home plate down the right-field line; its most distant stretches 421 feet in right-center. Almost immediately, sluggers embraced the ballpark, none more so than Barry Bonds, the Giants' outfielder who eclipsed baseball's all-time home-run record there on August 7, 2007.

The park has upscale accommodations (including 68 luxury suites, 5,200 club seats, and 1,500 field seats), but the views from each of the 41,500 seats are spectacular. These vistas include a huge sign featuring a Coca-Cola bottle pouring into an enormous baseball glove near the left-field bleachers. Both components of the ad arrived by barge.

The Giants excelled in their new park, capturing the NL West in 2000, their first season there. They went to the World Series in 2002, and won World Series titles in '10, '12, and '14.

Quirky field dimensions and the presence of McCovey Cove beyond the right-field fence are among the idiosyncrasies that make AT&T Park one of baseball's most beloved stadiums.

TIGER TOWN: COMERICA PARK

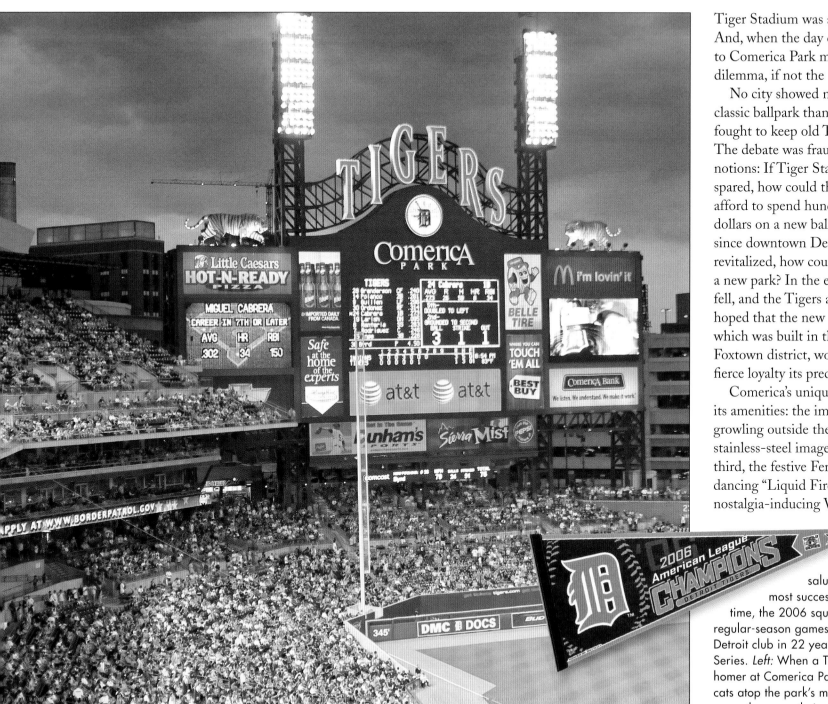

Tiger Stadium was a tough act to follow. And, when the day comes, the successor to Comerica Park may discover the same dilemma, if not the same uproar.

No city showed more affection for its classic ballpark than Detroit, whose fans fought to keep old Tiger Stadium alive. The debate was fraught with competing notions: If Tiger Stadium could not be spared, how could the cash-strapped city afford to spend hundreds of millions of dollars on a new ballpark? Conversely, since downtown Detroit needed to be revitalized, how could the city *not* afford a new park? In the end, Tiger Stadium fell, and the Tigers and Detroit fans hoped that the new Comerica Park, which was built in the city's downtown Foxtown district, would compel the same fierce loyalty its predecessor earned.

Comerica's uniqueness is illustrated by its amenities: the imposing tiger figures growling outside the gates, Ty Cobb's stainless-steel image sliding hard into third, the festive Ferris wheel, the dancing "Liquid Fireworks," and the nostalgia-inducing Walk of Fame.

Above: This pennant salutes Comerica Park's most successful team up to that time, the 2006 squad that won 95 regular-season games and became the first Detroit club in 22 years to reach the World Series. *Left:* When a Tigers player hits a homer at Comerica Park, the eyes of the two cats atop the park's massive scoreboard light up as they roar their approval.

A 15-foot-high tiger "welcoming" fans to the main gate of Comerica Park (and frequently serving as a photo backdrop) is one of nine Bengal statues featured throughout the stadium grounds.

Built for $300 million of mostly private money, Comerica Park sits alongside Ford Field (home of the NFL's Lions), an office building, and upscale housing. Unlike Tiger Stadium, which had double-deck outfield bleachers that dominated its vistas, Comerica Park offers open skyline views beyond its outfield walls. Stick-figure light towers, which are patterned after those at Cleveland's Jacobs Field, dot the awning above the upper deck. Above the 23,000-seat lower bowl, luxury suites extend to the foul poles and into outfield seating. In all, the ballpark holds just over 40,000 spectators.

Tigers' owner Mike Ilitch led the planning of the ballpark with HOK architects. The designs included a flagpole that sat in play amid the deepest regions of left-center field, a salute to the pole that once stood at old Tiger Stadium. The plans also included distant outfield fences, which made the ballpark a pitcher's best friend. But while having a home field that surrenders few long balls is good news for pitchers, it was bad news for ticket-sellers in the home-run-happy era. Right-handed hitters seemed especially troubled with Ilitch's vision; they squinted to see outfield fences that reached 420 feet in center field and 395 feet in left-center.

By 2003, the stadium had changed: The flagpole was moved off the field and the outfield fence in left-center was brought in 25 feet. The impact was immediate. Observers estimated that 99 home runs hit in the first two seasons with the new fence configuration would have been fly-outs in previous years. In 2005, the Tigers replaced the bullpens in right field with 950 bleacher seats; new bullpens were placed in the gap created by the shortened fences in left field.

In 2007, attendance at the Tigers' new home passed the three-million total for the first time. This mark came a season after the Tigers won the AL pennant, earning an spot in the World Series, which they lost to the St. Louis Cardinals. They returned to the World Series in 2012.

HOMETOWN HERO

TIGERS OWNER MIKE ILITCH could have sold out and made millions in profits. Instead, he showed a commitment to Detroit and its fans. In 2009, times in Detroit were tough—and the city's auto industry was especially hard-hit.

When General Motors, once the country's strongest corporation, fell into bankruptcy and could no longer afford to sponsor the "Liquid Fireworks" fountains at Comerica Park after nine seasons, Ilitch didn't allow someone else to pony up the estimated $2-million naming-rights fee.

Instead, Ilitch had the logos of GM, Chrysler, and Ford mounted above the scoreboard during the 2009 season as a show of support. Attached was a sign that read, "The Detroit Tigers support our automakers." At a time when ballplayers and owners were reaping millions while blue-collar workers were standing in unemployment lines and facing foreclosures, the gesture was a public-relations grand slam in the Motor City.

"It was a community decision and not a business decision," said team spokesperson Ron Colangelo. By the 2010 home opener, General Motors had returned as the fountain's sponsor.

MILLER TIME IN MILWAUKEE

Broken promises, construction delays, cost overruns, a recall election, even death—all surrounded Miller Park before the Brewers opened its doors. Such is the not-so-charming story of Milwaukee's modern ballpark odyssey.

Starting in the mid-1980s, Brewers owner Bud Selig spent a decade trying to build a new facility. First he pledged to pay for it himself, then he sought help from taxpayers. Despite the voters' rejection of his funding plan, Selig lobbied the state for financial aid. He received it, with the decisive vote coming from a state senator, George Petak; that

vote cost the Racine native his job, as his constituents made him the target of the state's first-ever recall election. The Brewers broke ground on the park in the fall of 1996.

In July 1999, with the park less than a year away from opening, a crane hoisting a 400-ton roof section collapsed, killing three workers. The unfinished ballpark sustained more than $100 million in damage (most of which was covered by insurance) in the accident. Still, the ballpark's price, originally budgeted at $250 million, rose to over $400 million after the costs of infrastructure improve-

ments were calculated. The Brewers funded a fraction of the additional cost, and nearly half of the difference was recouped by selling the ballpark's naming rights to Miller Beer.

In the end, the Brewers got a new 41,900-seat ballpark, retractable roof and all, to replace the outmoded and obsolete County Stadium, which sat across the parking lot until it was demolished. President

Above right: This Brewers program hailed the season attendance record set at Miller Park in 2007. It was a record that was broken the very next year, when three-million-plus turned out. Fans were rewarded with a Wild Card berth— the Brew Crew's first postseason appearance in 26 years. *Right:* Miller Park's 175-foot-high retractable roof was uniquely designed to include glass windows, which allow sunlight to reach the natural grass even when the roof is closed.

Wisconsinites love their tailgating, and Miller Park's spacious parking lots were built to accommodate plenty of pregame revelry, including brats, burgers, and beer.

George W. Bush tossed the ceremonial first pitch at Miller Park in 2001.

Despite its brick facade and structural elegance, early reviews of Miller Park were mixed. Some complained that its location—two miles from downtown—precluded the urban revitalization witnessed in other cities with new parks. Others missed mascot Bernie Brewer's slides into a giant mug of suds, which were beloved at County Stadium. Still others criticized the fan-shape roof—its awkward design, its high cost of maintenance, and its occasional leaks. On the upside, the glass windows incorporated in the roof's design provide openness and sunlight, which allows grass to grow.

Brewers fans are a tailgating bunch, and the Miller Park parking lots provide ample space for the roasting of brats, as well as portable toilets and places to stash hot ashes. Fans cheer a bratwurst, Polish sausage, Italian sausage, hot dog, and chorizo during the Klement's Famous Racing Sausages sprint.

Miller Park's first season saw the Brewers draw 2.8 million fans. Later, *Sports Illustrated* rated the park as baseball's best value for fans. Miller Park plays as a hitter's delight: So prevalent were home runs that a gas-pump counter that tallies dingers was added to the scoreboard during the 2007 season.

"It flies out of here," Brewers slugger Richie Sexson told reporters. "We're happy; the pitchers aren't." The "hitter's park" reputation has remained, and the Brewers have embraced it by filling their lineup with young sluggers such as Prince Fielder and Ryan Braun. In 2008, the team made its first playoff appearance in more than two decades. The Brewers drew more than three million fans in 2008, '09 and '11.

CUTTING THE MUSTARD

IT'S ONE OF life's great mysteries: Why do we watch adults dressed as sausages, pierogi, and presidents race around a ballpark? The world may never know.

This much we *do* know: We have the Milwaukee Brewers to thank for this baseball tradition. The Brewers' Famous Racing Sausages sprint began as an animated scoreboard competition in the early 1990s. Eventually, people in costumes raced instead of pixels. The original competitors were a bratwurst, a Polish sausage, and an Italian sausage; later, a hot dog and a chorizo were added to the recipe. At times, ballplayers don costumes to take part in the race. This on-field between-innings entertainment is a hit with kids and adults.

The sensation has spread around baseball. At first, many ballparks relied on video-board races. Fans, however, clamored for live action, so the Milwaukee model was followed instead. In Pittsburgh, they race pierogi. In Washington, four presidents run. In Cleveland and Kansas City, hot dogs with different condiments go at it. The list, like these races, runs ever on.

As was the case at County Stadium, no Miller Park game is complete without the Famous Racing Sausages. Pictured (from left) are Chorizo, Brat, Italian, Polish, and Hot Dog.

PIRATES HAVE A WINNER WITH PNC PARK

One summer in the mid-2000s, ESPN visited every major-league ballpark and ranked them on everything from their exterior facades to their hot dogs to their ushers. In Pittsburgh, all comparisons ended. Step aside Fenway, Wrigley, and Camden Yards—PNC Park set the standard. Thanks to its location on the Allegheny River, its reverence to history, its attention to detail, and the comfort delivered to its fans, Pittsburgh's park took the prize.

HOK designers did more than just copy the styles of classic venues and their retro descendants when planning PNC Park. The stadium, which was built for $262 million (including land acquisition), is a picturesque vision on the riverfront. Fans can approach on foot from the Roberto Clemente Bridge (which is pedestrian-only on game days). At the bridge's edge, they are met by shops, restaurants, and a sports pavilion with attractions for young and old alike.

The designers of PNC paid homage to Pittsburgh's first baseball palace, Forbes Field, when planning the facility. Archways at the entrance level greet fans, while decorative terra-cotta-tile pilasters and blue steel light posts stimulate memories of the former ballpark. PNC Park features a striking limestone facade topped by a green steel roof that partially covers a two-deck grandstand. This stadium's sight lines are unsurpassed. And with the most distant seat a mere 88

Its location on the Allegheny River is one of many reasons to rave about PNC Park, which gives Pirates fans a blend of old-time baseball and all the modern perks.

feet from the field, its confines are stunningly intimate.

Inside PNC Park, natural grass spans an asymmetrical outfield. A 21-foot fence in right field accommodates a scoreboard while a set of bleachers rises above the fence. Around the infield, limestone walls front the lower grandstand, providing a classic backdrop on TV. A striking view of the Pittsburgh skyline and the Clemente Bridge is revealed beyond the outfield fence.

Double-deck bleachers in left give way to one of baseball's most informative scoreboards. A ramp near the foul pole offers more than access to the upper deck—it gives fans immaculate views from four perches. Wide concourses give open perspectives all around the infield, which allow spectators to walk around and take in the game. The Riverwalk beyond the right-field fence is a popular destination. This outer promenade provides a unique panorama of the playing field and outstanding views of downtown Pittsburgh and the Allegheny River.

Sixty-nine luxury suites wrap the field, and club seating on two levels comes with its own lounges; there are 38,362 seats in all. The park offers a variety of food, including "Willie's Chili" in Pops Plaza (both of which are named in honor of Pirates legends Willie "Pops" Stargell), Pittsburgh's signature Primanti Brothers sandwiches,

and Manny's Bar-B-Q, which is run by former Bucs catcher Manny Sanguillen.

Great players from Pirates history are acknowledged by statues, some of which have moved from Forbes Field to Three Rivers Stadium and finally to PNC Park. Honus Wagner meets fans at the home-plate entrance, Clemente stands at the bridge named in his honor, and Willie Stargell's likeness is at the entrance in left field. A city street near the park is named in honor of Hall of Fame second baseman Bill Mazeroski.

After spending some 30 seasons at the concrete doughnut that was Three Rivers

Stadium, Pirates fans found PNC Park to be a breath of fresh air. On April 9, 2001, as fans mourned the death of Stargell (which occurred that morning), there weren't many dry eyes in the house when the new ballpark was unveiled.

Unfortunately for PNC fans, they watched the Pirates set a record for the longest streak of losing seasons in the history of North America's four major professional sports (1993–2102). Since that long slump, however, the Pirates put together three straight playoff seasons from '13 to '15.

Roberto Clemente is honored at PNC Park inside and out, from the stunning bridge named after him to a right-field wall that rises 21 feet, a measurement that honors the late Hall of Famer's jersey number (21).

CINCY'S GREAT AMERICAN ECHOES CROSLEY

Below: The Cincinnati Reds, the oldest franchise in professional baseball, debuted their new stadium on March 31, 2003, which this pennant commemorates. *Bottom:* Great American Ball Park is a riverfront stadium, but it's everything that Riverfront Stadium was not, from its natural grass to its wide variety of concessions and amenities.

For 17 summers, Reds captain Barry Larkin, a native Cincinnatian, toiled on the often-blistering artificial turf that was rolled over the concrete of Riverfront Stadium. This hardship was over, finally, when Cincinnati's Great American Ball Park opened on March 31, 2003.

"This ballpark is beautiful," Larkin gushed like a rookie to *The Cincinnati Enquirer.* "There's definitely some character here."

Compared to the faceless round concrete slab that was Riverfront Stadium, Great American Ball Park was a welcome sight. It wasn't easy, though—building the new field

was a ten-year trek from conception to first pitch.

Like many teams at the onset of the ballpark construction boom, the Reds were stuck in an outmoded facility that failed to generate cash flow through high-price suites, club seating, and generous advertising contracts. Both the Reds and the NFL's Bengals sought a divorce from Riverfront provided they could secure separate sport-specific venues. Ultimately, Queen City citizens made the Reds' baseball-only gem a reality, first by agreeing to pay for it through taxes and then by ensuring its idyllic location on the banks of the Ohio River, where it stands along Sawyer Point and Yeatman's Cove as the centerpiece of

an ambitious economic-development plan for the downtown area.

In many ways, Great American Ball Park's design borrows from Crosley Field. Unlike the simple Crosley, however, Great American came with a $280-million price tag and seating for just over 42,000. Fans and players alike loved the new facility, but some critics claimed that it tried too hard to satisfy too many.

Real grass—five varieties of perennial ryegrass—is grown on site. Exposed white steel contrasts nicely with the sweep of red seats. A dozen toothbrush-shape steel-supported light towers dot the ballpark. Mosaics recognizing the 1869 Reds (baseball's first professional team) and the mighty Big Red Machine

A pair of riverboat smokestacks in right-center field, which call to mind Cincinnati's history of steamships, send fireworks into the air whenever a Reds player socks a home run.

FINDLAY MARKET'S OPENING DAY TRADITION

ON APRIL 17, 1889—Opening Day—the Cincinnati Orchestra greeted an estimated 15,000 fans at League Park. That day, a tradition was born. Historians aren't sure why Cincinnati was bestowed the honor of hosting baseball's first game each year, but some believe that it is because the city was home to the Red Stockings, baseball's first professional team.

Save for the 1966 and 1990 seasons, Cincinnati has hosted each Opening Day. In 1966, three straight rainouts forced the Reds to open on the road.; in 1990, a lockout delayed the start of the season, so the Reds opened the campaign in Houston.

Opening Day is a holiday in the Queen City. A parade—featuring bands, floats, and fireworks—seems to have always been a part of the attraction. Beginning in 1920, the annual event started at Findlay Market. In the late 1980s, during owner Marge Schott's era, zoo animals became part of the celebration.

"There are a lot of good Opening Days, but it's tough to top those elephants in Cincinnati," said former Reds player Lenny Harris.

A Pete Rose mascot marches in the 2003 Findlay Market Parade.

of the 1970s greet spectators at the main gate. In right field, an isolated bleacher section sits near the park's most unique features: a pair of riverboat smokestacks that fire for Cincinnati home runs and two steel light towers that evoke memories of Crosley Field.

Reds history is prominently featured throughout the ballpark. Crosley Terrace features statues of Ted Kluszewski, Ernie Lombardi, Joe Nuxhall, and Frank Robinson. Banners that hang all around salute historic moments.

The new park's playing dimensions are intentionally similar to those of Crosley. Like Crosley, for example, Great

American has a 12-foot wall in left field that sits 328 feet from home plate. Beyond the fence is the park's 68-foot-high scoreboard, which is topped by a clock that recalls the one at Crosley. A "black-glass box" in Great American's center field, 404 feet from home, serves as a batter's background but also holds a party room. In right, an eight-foot wall stands 325 feet from home plate; it is as short a porch as is allowed by Major League Baseball. Sluggers found a paradise, while fantasy baseball enthusiasts quickly learned to avoid Cincy pitchers. "I'd love to hit in this ballpark," Reds legend Johnny Bench said.

SAN DIEGO'S GREAT LOCATION: PETCO PARK

Right: San Diego's historic Gaslamp Quarter was known for its nightlife even before Petco Park took summer nights to a new level when it opened in 2004. *Below:* Thanks to its spacious field dimensions, Petco is a pitcher-friendly venue. Between its opening and the 2012 season, when the fences were moved in slightly, Petco yielded the fewest number of runs in all of baseball.

Success in the San Diego real estate market comes down to location, location, location. The centerpiece of the city's historic waterfront Gaslamp Quarter district, Petco Park opened in 2004 to effusive reviews; it was hailed as an architectural masterpiece and the key to the neighborhood's renaissance.

San Diego's Gaslamp Quarter dates back to the 19th century, when the city was booming and Wyatt Earp ran the neighborhood gambling house. After World War II, the Quarter fell into disarray as urban sprawl took hold. Petco Park designers didn't forget the neighborhood's history. In much the same way that a railroad warehouse is featured at Camden Yards, planners incorporated the long-abandoned Western Metal Supply Co. building right into Petco

Park's left-field corner. Its painted white lettering is visible from most areas of the park. There are 180 seats on its roof, and inside are two floors of chic specialty suites with balconies that overlook the diamond, as well as a top-floor lounge. A team souvenir shop can be found at field level.

Petco Park is named for a chain of pet supply stores, a fact that led to early nicknames like "Bark Park" and "Animal House." Every detail was carefully planned to ensure that the Padres' new park blends with and bolsters its surroundings. Its facade is adorned with imported Indian sandstone to reflect nearby sandy beaches and cliffs. Inside the park, one sees a sea of 42,000 navy-blue seats, as well as vistas of San Diego Bay, the city skyline, and Balboa Park. Even the white-painted exposed steel is intended to evoke images of watercraft floating in the bay. Erik Judson, former Padres' vice-president of development, said the Padres wanted "a ballpark that looks and feels like San Diego."

Petco Park's arrival was slow in coming. For many years, former Padres owner John Moores had sought a more intimate and profitable home than Qualcomm Stadium. Even after ground was broken, the new park was beset by scandals, delays, and lawsuits. In fact, for one 15-month spell, all work on the half-completed ballpark came to a halt. Finally, in 2004—after more than five years had passed since voters approved a ballot measure to fund the $450-million ballpark—Petco opened for business.

Visitors can hop aboard the San Diego Trolley, a bus, a train, a water taxi, a ferry, or even a pedicab to get to the ballpark. With a $15 lawn seat, fans young and old can romp the rolling grass of the 2.7-acre "Park at the Park" beyond center field. This area includes a mammoth video screen that allows fans to watch the game while children run around a playground or build sand castles on the manufactured beach. On the other side of the fence that supports the screen is the "Jury Box," a small set of bleachers that bends into

right field along the foul line. Upper-deck seating, which at most new ballparks puts fans farther away from the field than they were at older stadiums, is actually closer at Petco than at Qualcomm thanks to a modern cantilevering design.

Petco Park quickly gained a reputation as a pitcher's palace, as hitters struggled to break through the thick salty air. In the first-ever series at Petco, the Padres and the Giants combined for a single home run in 214 at-bats. San Diego slugger Ryan Klesko was frustrated after smack-

ing a ground-rule double and two long fly balls that fell innocently into an outfielder's mitt. "Anywhere else in the National League and I'm 3-for-3 with three homers," he told reporters.

This frustration may have been overstated. The Padres hit 11 more team home runs in that first year than they did in their last at Qualcomm. San Diego fans, meanwhile, saw their team's ERA dip by nearly a run a game. Eventually, the Padres adjusted and captured back-to-back division titles in 2005 and '06.

Petco's left-field foul "pole" is a painted yellow stripe on the southeast corner of the renovated Western Metal Supply Co. building, 336 feet from home plate.

PHILLIES STOP THE BOOS AT "THE BANK"

Boos showered down from a half-empty upper deck almost as if they were racing the chilled raindrops that splashed onto Philadelphia's new baseball park on Opening Day. Chants of "Let's Go Flyers" filled the air. Jeers at a home opener? Cheers for a hockey team? It could only happen in Philly. Indeed, the city's supposed brotherly love rarely extends to its sports teams. "You can't get on the fans," former Phillies manager Larry Bowa said. "They can boo. They're frustrated. They want to see a winner."

This is how Citizens Bank Park was christened on April 12, 2004. Fortunately for everyone's sanity, there were much better days ahead for the Phillies and their new home—the team would soon reach baseball's pinnacle, and its stadium would win acclaim as one of the most exquisite embodiments of the "retro-classic" ballpark era.

Situated at 11th and Pattison, the $346-million facility was publicly and privately financed. It rose in the shadow of the sterile Veterans Stadium, which had been the home to the Phils since 1971. Citizens, popularly called "The Bank," holds more than 43,000 fans in a seating arrangement inspired by the Baker Bowl and Shibe Park—the Phillies' former homes—where the upper and lower decks sometimes didn't connect and the cantilevered design provided open seating areas. To evoke more nostalgia, 300 rooftop bleacher seats, similar to those sold at old Shibe Park, are available. Citizens has a triple-deck grandstand in right field and a natural-grass turf. Luxury suites can be leased for seven or ten years at a time.

The ballpark's facade is composed of red steel, brick, and stone. Ten-foot-tall bronze statues of Hall of Famers Mike Schmidt, Steve Carlton, Robin Roberts, and Richie Ashburn stand at the entrances. Behind center field, The Bank features "Ashburn Alley," which offers a range of Philadelphia cuisine and retail shopping spots, as well as the "All-Star Walk," a path that pays tribute to Phillies All-Stars. Fans who want to remember yesteryear can visit "Memory Lane," an illustrated history of Philadelphia baseball that spotlights the Phillies, the Athletics, and the city's Negro League teams. Philly fans can take out their frustrations on opposing pitchers who are warming up in the upper bullpen, which is adjacent to the Alley. Originally, the upper pen was meant for Phillie flingers, but a switch was made after heckling fans caused too much grief for the hometown hurlers.

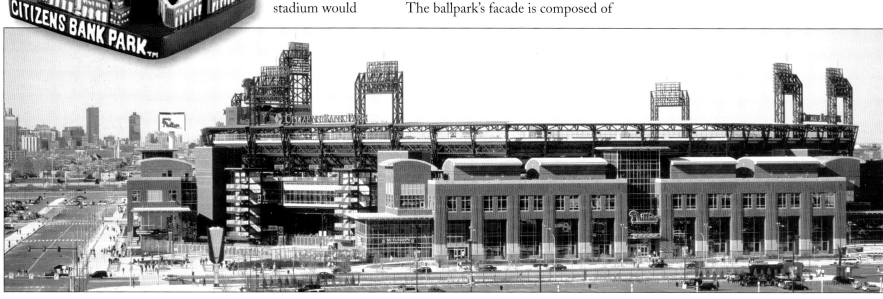

A replica of the Liberty Bell stands 100 feet above the outfield; it lights up and tolls for every Phillies homer. And there were dingers aplenty that first season, as Phils hitters cranked 49 more homers than in 2003 at the Vet, topping the 200 mark for the first time in team history. Long balls were so common that in 2006 the left-field power-alley fence was pushed back five feet to 374 feet and raised to ten-and-a-half feet.

The park's left-center-field wall sits, at its farthest, about 409 feet from home plate; it is aptly named "The Angle." At Washington's Griffith Stadium, a similar outfield wall was bent to accommodate trees that grew outside the park; in Philadelphia, The Angle was added for quirkiness. The fence has heights that taper from 19 feet to nearly 13 feet. Balls that are hit off the wall shoot back toward the field in all sorts of directions.

The Phillies have found success at their new ballpark. In 2008, they hushed The Bank's boo-birds (at least temporarily) by winning their first World Series since 1980.

Citizens Bank Park offers views of Philadelphia's skyline and rooftop bleachers, which bring back memories of Shibe Park for some.

NEW BUSCH IS CLOSE TO HARDBALL HEAVEN

Of the many great views from Busch Stadium in St. Louis, none is more prominent than that of the famed Gateway Arch, the city's greatest landmark.

In St. Louis, fans like to say that baseball heaven opened its gates in the spring of 2006 when shiny new Busch Stadium was unveiled. And it certainly appeared as though the gods of the national pastime were smiling on the Gateway City, as every red seat seemed stuffed for every contest that first season, right up to the clinching game of the World Series.

The Cardinals' 2006 season was a campaign for the ages: The inauguration of a new ballpark served as a prelude to an unlikely championship run. Twenty minutes after Cards closer Adam Wainwright fired strike three past Tiger Brandon Inge to clinch the title, St. Louis fans were still whooping it up inside Busch Stadium. "I'm looking around at all the confetti, and the fans are still here," Wainwright said. "This is such a great town and a great team. We fought so hard to be here. We deserve it, and they deserve it."

The Cardinals and their fans also deserved the new Busch Stadium. The club is one of baseball's most storied franchises, ranking behind only the Yankees in terms of World Series titles. Since 1966, the Redbirds had played at Busch Memorial Stadium, which was built as a multipurpose facility but rarely hosted anything other than baseball after the NFL's Cardinals left town in 1988.

When the new Busch Stadium was proposed, the Cardinals had visions of a development called "Ballpark Village" that would jump-start a new downtown neighborhood. As is the case with many proposed ballparks, controversy boiled over the funding of the $365-million palace. In the end, the facility was privately financed, save for a government loan. There was no debate over the city's need for an economic boost, however—nicknamed the "Gateway to the West,"

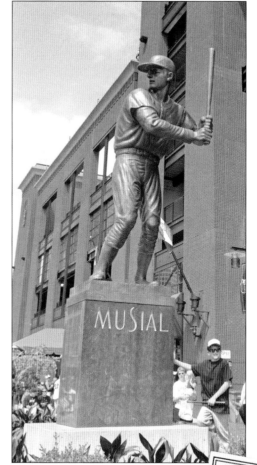

St. Louis had seen its population decline over five decades, a trend that was symbolized by a listless downtown.

The opening of Busch Stadium promised to change the mood of the city. And indeed, by the time the ballpark opened, the former garment-district neighborhood—with its upscale condos, shops, and restaurants—was already in the midst of a transformation; in point of fact, the population in the city and downtown has risen in recent years.

And as promised, Busch Stadium was pure St. Louis in terms of character, history, and style. Its red-brick facade with arched passages and an exposed steel canopy complement the nearby Cupples Station warehouses and the historic Wainwright Building (coincidentally enough). The ballpark's pedestrian walkway and the steel incorporated into the exterior are fashioned after the nearby Eads Bridge, which spans the Mississippi River. The walkway leads to an entrance that bears the pennants of St. Louis's championship clubs and a statue of Hall of Famer Stan "The Man" Musial. With its natural-grass field resting below street level and no grandstand blocking the view, the buildings of the St. Louis skyline—most notably the fabled Gateway Arch—rise impressively beyond the green outfield fences.

After old Busch Stadium was bulldozed, Clark Street was reopened, giving some a free peek inside the new ballpark from knotholes in fences beyond the outfield. While the outfield dimensions are similar to those of old Busch Memorial, new Busch's foul-ball areas are smaller, which allows lower-deck seats to be at least 40 feet closer to the infield. All 50,000-plus seats are colored Cardinal red. A retro clock with two cardinals perched above a Budweiser sign sits atop the right-field scoreboard.

Cards fans embraced the new ballpark, buying 3.4 million tickets that first season in the venue. The Cardinals responded with a mediocre 83 wins, which was still enough to win the mediocre NL Central. The Redbirds caught fire in October, however, and ended up winning the World Series.

NATIONALS PARK HAS MODERN DESIGNS

A unique design of steel, glass, and concrete ensures that Nationals Park fits in nicely with some of the well-known architecture in the nation's capital.

Once orphaned and then adopted by the other 29 major-league teams, the Washington Nationals finally found a real home on the northwest bank of the Anacostia River.

Six times in baseball history, Washingtonians had watched ball teams come and go—the last departure occurred when the Senators moved to Arlington, Texas, in 1972. But when Ryan Zimmerman smacked a walk-off home run at the new Nationals Park on March 30, 2008, it became clear that the Nats had finally settled into the comforts of a stable environment.

The Nats were once the Montreal Expos, a poorly financed franchise for which no buyer could be found. But

instead of contracting the franchise as threatened, baseball owners collectively bought in, taking over operations while agreeing to move the club to Washington for the 2005 season. The relocation was contingent on the construction of a new ballpark, but gaining approval for funding for the stadium proved difficult. While most Washington voters disapproved of the proposed financing plan, the D.C. City Council—with the backing of Mayor Anthony Williams—pushed the deal through. Of the approved $611-million price (it ended up costing more), baseball owners would chip in a paltry $20 million.

After it opened, Nationals Park was met with ho-hum reviews. Its riverbank location was seen as a potential boon to a

long-suffering neighborhood; ancillary development, unfortunately, has been slow in coming.

Ballpark designers opted for a modern design—incorporating glass, precast concrete, and steel—that emulates D.C.'s stately public buildings. The stadium can seat more than 41,000, and spectators are provided panoramic riverfront views of the Navy Yard and, in the distance, the U.S. Capitol and the Washington Monument. The East Wing of the National Gallery of Art, which was designed by renowned architect I. M. Pei, served as inspiration for the design.

Nationals Park has a natural playing surface that lies some 24 feet below street level; in fact, most spectators walk straight to their seats without using ramps or elevators. For the affluent, the ballpark offers club seating and 78 luxury suites—some of which are named for former U.S. presidents and adorned with leather chairs, marble-top tables, porcelain floors, and 42-inch flat-screen TVs.

The concourse features padded pillars that bear images of great players and local heroes, such as former Senator slugger Frank Howard and Hall of Famer Jackie Robinson. The diamond opens to an asymmetrical outfield that includes an oddly shaped jog along the right-center-field fence that is meant to evoke memories of the long-gone Griffith Stadium. And while it took the Nationals a while to build a winner on the field, their ballpark is the first major stadium to be honored by the United States Green Building Council.

For fun, Nationals Park stages a "Presidents Race" in the middle of the fourth inning; in it, caricatures of George Washington, Thomas Jefferson, Abraham Lincoln, and Teddy Roosevelt sprint for superiority. The Nats, meanwhile, are still attempting to involve themselves in a *pennant* race.

Above: Since most seats are at street level or below, there's little climbing to do at Nationals Park. The climb Washington fans now clamor for is in the NL East standings. *Right:* An inauguration in D.C. usually takes place only once every four years. Though they moved from Montreal in 2004, the Nats inaugurated their new venue in 2008, as lauded by this patch.

JOSH GIBSON HONORED BY NATIONALS

HE WAS THE greatest slugger who never played in a major-league game; his skin color was the only reason. History, however, honors Josh Gibson and his team, the Homestead Grays. The club originated in the Pittsburgh suburb of Homestead in 1912 and later barnstormed the country.

The Grays joined the Negro National League (NNL) in 1935 and split their home games between Pittsburgh's Forbes Field and Washington's Griffith Stadium. Through the years, the team boasted several of the best African American players of the era, including Gibson, "Cool Papa" Bell, and Buck Leonard. As a result, the Grays won nine consecutive NNL pennants from 1937 to 1945.

A burly catcher, Gibson is considered by many to have been the greatest Negro League position player. His round-trippers were legendary, and he is believed to have led the Negro Leagues in home runs nearly every year from 1930 to 1945. In 1947, he died of a stroke at age 35, three months before Jackie Robinson's major-league debut; he entered baseball's Hall of Fame in 1972. Nationals Park has honored Gibson—along with Senators greats Walter Johnson and Frank Howard—with a statue.

CITI FIELD PAYS HOMAGE TO NEW YORK'S PAST

When the Mets were born in 1962, they inherited pieces of the departed Dodgers and Giants franchises, with a smidgen of the Yankees thrown in. Mets caps borrowed their "NY" insignias from the Giants, the team's blue and orange colors were those of both the Giants and the Dodgers, and their pinstripes mimicked those of the Yankees. What's more, their roster that dreadful first season included castoffs from all three teams.

So when it came time to design Citi Field—which replaced dilapidated Shea Stadium as the home of the Mets in 2009—the team borrowed the face of Brooklyn's Ebbets Field, perhaps the most beloved ballpark ever. And all around Citi Field, the Mets show proper reverence to New York baseball history while showcasing modern marvels and providing necessities that were just rumors at Shea.

Citi Field's $800-million sticker price shocked many New Yorkers, particularly because they would be footing most of the bill. Additionally, the naming rights to the ballpark were sold to Citigroup just before its role in the nation's banking crisis was exposed. Still, most Mets fans—at least those who can afford the expensive tickets—enjoy its comforts, theme-park atmosphere, and amenities. Many call it the "Anti-Shea."

Built in the shadow of Shea, Citi Field is a natural-grass ballpark designed by Populous, the former HOK Sport group. The stunning venue includes 41,800 dark-green seats, all of which face the infield. Fans who arrive on the elevated No. 7 train pass through a handsomely decorated plaza to the ballpark's numerous arched windows, which bend into a grand brick facade. At the main gate is the park's signature rotunda, which is named in honor of Jackie Robinson.

Exposed dark-blue structural steel finished in a bridgelike motif is prominent throughout the park. The same steel composes trusses, traditional light towers, and the roof's canopy, which evokes an elevated train stop. A

Far left: Though Citi Field's capacity is dwarfed by that of Shea Stadium, the large crowds that show up are treated to immaculate conditions, amazing sight lines, and wonderful amenities. *Left:* This patriotic souvenir baseball was offered to celebrate the first games at Citi Field, a pair of exhibition contests in 2009 that pitted the Mets against the Red Sox.

Great Mets players and moments from the past adorn the outside of Citi Field. Among the milestones memorialized are the club's 1969 and 1986 World Series titles.

A TALE OF ONE CITY

CITI FIELD TRIES to be a ballpark for all New Yorkers, be they fans of Ebbets Field or the Polo Grounds—or even Shea Stadium.

While its classic brick facade is clearly linked—at least in spirit—to that of Ebbets Field, the park's dimensions and seating are far more modern. Its deep outfield alleys, the home-run Big Apple, and the roars of jets flying overhead remind one of Shea. Many of the things that made Ebbets Field charming—the nooks, the zany bounces off an outfield fence—were left out of Citi Field's designs; not so the famed Ebbets rotunda, however.

To pay homage to the Giants and the Polo Grounds, there is an orange stripe that runs along Citi Field's outfield wall and the up park's foul poles. Otherwise, New York baseball fans who yearn for the good old days have found no links to the Giants in the Mets' new stadium, despite the fact that the Mets' first home was abandoned by the team that took New York's heart to San Francisco.

Ebbets Field (top) and Citi Field have eerie similarities.

pedestrian bridge—a miniature version of the Hell Gate Bridge—spans the bullpen behind right-center field.

Citi Field's spectator-pleasing openness is a product of expansive concourses that open to the playing field and provide peeks of Queens and Flushing Bay. In some spots, fans can even espy the Manhattan skyline. From the visitors' bullpen, one can see timeworn buildings and shops along 126th Street. While its dimensions are similar to those of Shea, a porch seating 1,200 shoots into fair territory in right field, a design that was modeled after the stands at old Tiger Stadium. Beneath the overhang, things get no easier for outfielders: The fence rises from eight feet at the foul pole to 18 feet under the porch.

Paradise awaits kids beyond center field, where they'll find Mr. Met's Kiddie Field—a scale replica of Citi Field—along with batting cages and other distractions. The nine-foot apple that rose and lit up for Mets home runs at Shea resides in a concourse, while a new, larger model sits poised behind Citi's center-field wall.

With fewer seats and a disappointing team, attendance actually fell from more than four million in 2008 to just over three million that first season at Citi Field. The Mets still managed to finish fifth in the NL in attendance, however.

NEW YANKEE STADIUM REPLACES A LEGEND

When it's time for one of their legends to move on, the Yankees somehow always have another waiting in the wings—from the Babe to Gehrig, DiMaggio to Mantle, Reggie to Winfield, and Mattingly to Jeter. The same is true of the team's homes: As one historic venue fell, "The House That George Would Build" rose to replace it.

In 2009, the stadium baton was passed as aging Yankees owner George Steinbrenner looked on, fighting his emotions. Just as the Yankees rarely miss a beat in maintaining their amazing dynasty, their new ballpark follows suit, echoing the past while acknowledging the future.

With Citi Field, the Mets' new ballpark, debuting at the same time, comparisons were inevitable. "Shea was

old when it was new, and the old Yankee Stadium never got old," Tim McCarver said. "You could have gone on and on and on with the old Yankee Stadium."

New Yankee Stadium was built for $1.5 billion during a huge national economic downturn. Tax-exempt bonds were sold to finance the ballpark, which means that the Yankees will pay for it over time. Taxpayers were also asked to assume some of the burden. More bad news

came when the price of the average ticket was revealed to be triple the cost of those in other cities. Furthermore, a "Legends Suite" infield seat was priced at $2,600. These mind-boggling figures led one fan to dub the park "The House That Loot Built." Regardless, the 30-month construction project, overseen by architects from Populous (the former HOK Sport group), ended with a near replica of the original 1923 stadium.

New Yankee Stadium sits just off Babe Ruth Plaza. Its facade, with limestone and granite surrounding sky-reaching arched windows, commands respect. Above the main gate, the words "Yankee Stadium" are etched in imitation gold and flanked by bronze eagle medallions. Inside, fans are greeted by broad open-air concourses, a welcome contrast to the cramped confines of the old

ballpark. Oversize posters of Yankee legends hang all around the Great Hall, which is located at the 31,000-square-foot main gate. The Yankees Museum displays team memorabilia.

Circling the grandstand roof is the ballpark's trademark frieze, a throwback to an aspect of the original stadium that essentially disappeared during the renovations of the 1970s. Perched above the frieze are the flags of all 30 major-league teams.

New Yankee Stadium is 63 percent larger than its predecessor, but it manages to feel more intimate due to its 50,000-plus seats offering enhanced sight lines. As at old Yankee Stadium, grandstand seating reaches around the foul poles before giving way to outfield bleachers. Fans can fill four levels, but a majority of the park's seats are located in its lower bowl. The Kentucky bluegrass outfield ends at the warning track in front of fences that stand the same distances from home as at old Yankee Stadium, but seats encroach closer at the new facility.

Monument Park, the tribute to great Yankees of the past, moved from the old stadium to the new one and sits beyond center field with the old park's home plate. Above it looms the center-field high-definition scoreboard, which is 59 feet high and 101 feet wide.

During the new stadium's first season in 2009, a barrage of 237 home runs was hit. A study concluded that the shape and height of the right-field wall—and not a wind tunnel, as had been speculated—might have propelled the binge. Some consider the onslaught a mere fluke. Regardless, the Yankees honored the new stadium with a World Series championship that first fall. At the beginning of the 2010 season, Derek Jeter and Manager Joe Girardi visited the owner's suite and personally presented George Steinbrenner his seventh (and final) ring as owner. Tradition carries on.

The Yankees' first season in their new stadium wound up with the club in a familiar spot: atop the American League in attendance and clutching a World Series trophy.

TARGET FIELD A HIT WITH THE TWINS

Above: After his first visit to Target Field, longtime Atlanta Braves manager Bobby Cox said "If I was going to build one, I'd build it just like this." *Right:* Kirby Puckett Jr. stands behind statues that honor his late father, a Twins great and Minnesota fan favorite, at Target Field before an April 2010 game.

Thanks to the opening of Target Field in 2010, the Twins were able to leave the dank confines of the Metrodome to catch a breath of fresh air and a few rays of sunshine.

After 28 summers spent indoors—during which the Twins won seven division titles and two World Series championships—the team moved into Target Field in downtown Minneapolis's warehouse district and began to enjoy the outdoors. The ballpark's construction came after much haggling and even the threat that the team would be contracted out of existence. It took more than 20 years of pleas for a better venue from the Twins, but eventually the new stadium was built at a cost of $522 million, with both private and public money being used for funding.

Target Field uses locally mined limestone in a not-so-retro, not-so-modern design. It blends nicely with its surroundings, including the nearby intermodal Target Field train station. Another product of the architects of Populous (formerly known as HOK Sport group), the ballpark accommodates 39,500 fans. Unlike its weather-wary contemporaries in Milwaukee and Seattle, Target has no retractable roof. The playing field includes sensors that turn on heat to help

grass grow, and the grandstand has climate-controlled areas to which fans can escape in the event of inclement weather. An enlarged canopy soffit tops the roof to provide some protection from the unpredictable Minnesota weather.

Like many new ballparks, Target Field respects baseball history. Its gates are designated using the uniform numbers of the Twins' greatest players—Rod Carew (29), Kirby Puckett (34), Harmon Killebrew (3), Tony Oliva (6), and Kent Hrbek (14)—plus national hero Jackie Robinson (42, of course). The venue also recognizes Twins history with a modernized version of the "Minnie and Paul Shaking Hands" logo of the 1960s, which rises above center field; after every Twin homer, the sign lights up with strobes. Trees compliment the outfield setting. Knotholes provide peeks from the 5th Street side of the park. Kentucky bluegrass mercifully replaces the knee-destroying artificial turf of the old dome.

Nearly half of the ballpark's dark-green seats are in the lower deck. The main three-tier grandstand curls from home plate to both foul poles; between the decks are 4,000 club seats and 54 luxury suites. A double-deck grandstand is located in left field; above it stands a massive scoreboard. A rising deck sits in right field. All of the stadium's seats face home plate. Beyond the outfield is the downtown Minneapolis skyline.

Target Field is viewed as something of a pitcher's park, unlike the old venue, the "Homerdome." From home plate to the fence in dead center field is 404 feet. The park's shortest porch is 328 feet to right, where a 23-foot wall runs from the foul pole to right-center field.

The Twins opened their ballpark on April 12, 2010, with a 5–2 win over Boston. That day, Minnesota fans began lining up at 6 A.M. to get a glimpse of their new second home. Scalpers sold tickets for several times their face value. Minnesota players, meanwhile, lavished praise on their new work area.

By the middle of their inaugural season of 2010 at Target Field, the Twins had sold enough tickets to put them over the three million mark for the year.

Now that outdoor baseball is back in Minnesota, the Twins hope to avoid the kind of weather that had Metropolitan Stadium manager Bill Williams (right) and groundskeeper Dick Ericson skating on March 25, 1965.

SNOWBALL, INDOORS OR OUT

THE TWINS DECIDED not to put a retractable roof on Target Field. Prior to the facility's opening, it had been a while since the team had been exposed to the capricious Minnesota climate. Weather in the area is always burdensome, from snow and rain in April to humid afternoons in July and August.

Minnesota baseball started with no protection. Nicollet Park was a cozy venue that first hosted the Western League's Minneapolis Millers in 1896 and the American Association's version of the team from 1902 through 1955. In 1933, slugger Joe Hauser hit his minor-league-record 69th home run there, but a rainout killed his shot at slugging No. 70.

In 1956, Metropolitan Stadium rose out of a cornfield, and after the 1960 season, the Millers faded away as the Twins arrived via Washington for the 1961 season. On April 12, 1965, Twins pitcher Jim Kaat was stranded outside the city due to a snowstorm and had to arrive at the Met via helicopter. The Twins would call the Met home through 1981. But even the roofed Metrodome was not immune to the elements: A 1983 game was postponed due to snow accumulation on the roof.

MARLINS PARK AN ART MUSEUM

Marlins Park has given Miami's Little Havana neighborhood a distinct look—and a South Florida feel. The stadium opened in 2012 on the spot where the Orange Bowl stood for more than 70 years.

A "surprise" storm while the retractable roof was agape on Opening Day 2015 soaked the field before a game against the Braves, forcing the first rain delay in the brief history of Marlins Park. It lasted just 16 minutes until the roof was closed, but it had Miami Marlins owner Jeffrey Loria sitting in disbelief with his head in his hands. "I thought we had a roof," Loria quipped to his club president, David Samson.

They do, of course, have a roof. And an impressive four-year-old stadium that includes aquariums behind home plate, a swimming pool, free wifi and some of the best food choices in the Majors—among other amenities. The park, resembling some kind of space-age cruise ship on the former site of the Orange Bowl in the Little Havana neighborhood, cannot remove the human error of misreading the weather radar on one particular Opening Day. However, just about everything else seems to be possible in one of the Major Leagues' newest attractions.

Even when the roof is closed—the norm in the sweltering South Florida summer—there are stunning views of the Miami skyline through 60-foot-tall windows. Two 450-gallon aquariums and the outfield swimming pool (inside a night club) provide a distinct Miami flair, as does a tribute to the Orange Bowl that includes reproductions of that stadium's old letters. A 360-degree promenade level ensures that fans never have to miss a pitch, even while ordering ceviche, a Cuban sandwich, or a plate of tacos.

"A lot of us weren't expecting something this nice," 38-year-old Miami native Adam Brownstein told the *New York Times* when the stadium opened in 2012.

Perhaps that had something to do with the team's old home. Sun Life Stadium, formerly Joe Robbie Stadium, is primarily a football venue. It was adjusted to support baseball in time for the Marlins' arrival as an expansion team in 1993, but it was never going to compete with the new, state-of-the-art, "retro-feeling," baseball-only parks that would spring open to rave reviews in cities like Cleveland, Seattle, Pittsburgh, and many others in the late 1990s and early 2000s.

In fact, Major League Baseball took it a giant step further. Not only was Sun Life less than ideal as a baseball venue; according to the powers-that-be, it needed to be replaced or Miami risked losing its team. A battle ensued over funding until the parties came to an agreement in 2007. The $634 million project—$515 million for the stadium itself—was funded mostly with taxpayer money, with the Marlins also kicking in more than $150 million.

Building was delayed by a lawsuit challenging the public funding. Finally, after 33 months of construction, the Marlins celebrated the grand opening on April 4, 2012, with a loss to the St. Louis Cardinals. The park's capacity of 37,000 is among the smallest in the Majors. But with the trouble the team has had drawing fans over the years, "cozy" suits the franchise just fine.

If the intimate venue is state-of-the-art, from its eco-friendly retractable roof to its massive, high-definition scoreboards, it is also a showcase for art—actual art. Marlins Park doubles as an art museum of sorts. Loria is an avid art collector and dealer, and it shows in the décor. World-renowned artists have their paintings and sculptures displayed around the stadium—a nod to the area's Art in Public Places program.

The pièce de résistance, so to speak, sits just left of center field and has polarized fans like few other spectacles in baseball. It's a $2.5 million sculpture by well-known pop artist Red Grooms. It lights up and springs into motion every time a Marlins player socks a home run.

Marlins fly, other fish bob in the water, and seagulls soar around the sun in a display unlike any other home run tradition in baseball. Grooms, from Nashville, said he drew inspiration from childhood trips to Daytona Beach, recalling the excitement of seeing the ocean. Home Run Sculpture is the official name, but patrons have called it any number of things—not all of them printable. "That thing out there is pretty garish. I'm not sure what it is," said Lance Berkman of the Cardinals at the grand opening. "The stadium itself is really pretty. I enjoyed the architecture."

What no fan can argue is that Marlins Park offers a South Beach flavor

Marlins Park's retractable roof is not only one of the best-functioning of its kind, it's also historic in its eco-friendliness. Having followed a comprehensive sustainability strategy through its design and construction, it became the first retractable structure to ever earn LEED Gold Certification from the U.S. Green Building Council.

everywhere you turn. From 200-foot LED columns that flicker in rhythm to music, to the DJ-infused club scene of The Clevelander, to the vibrant colors everywhere and truly international dining options—with a Cuban flair, of course—the stadium reflects its surroundings in an authentic if somewhat kitschy way.

"It's lively, it's entertaining, and it's so Miami," said former Marlins relief pitcher Heath Bell.

Though the Marlins don't exactly have the national following of teams like the Yankees, Red Sox or Dodgers and have struggled to fill the seats, baseball fans around the world got a chance to check out their distinctive park during the 2017 Major League All-Star Game. And what an exciting showcase they witnessed, as Robinson Cano won it for the American League on the first extra-inning home run in an All-Star Game since 1967.

"More important than the $100 million in economic benefit, more important than the 75,000 rooms in our hotels, more important than the viewing audience throughout the world is that this game is of great importance for the soul of the City of Miami," said Miami mayor Tomas Regalado.

Added Loria: "The future is bright for Miami and its baseball fans."

Bright indeed. And colorful. And, on most days, delightfully dry.

Perhaps the best "seats" in the house at Marlins Park belong to the fish occupying two 450-gallon, saltwater aquariums behind home plate. A material called Lexan, used in bullet-proof glass, protects the gilled occupants from foul balls and errant pitches.

BRAVES MOVE INTO MAJORS' NEWEST MASTERPIECE

Above: Though SunTrust's capacity is about 9,000 less than that of Turner, the new stadium in the Majors offers a fan experience that its predecessor couldn't approach.

After just two decades of largely great baseball at Turner Field, the Atlanta Braves moved to the suburbs (technically where Atlanta *meets* the suburbs in neighboring Cobb County) in 2017. And the newest park in the majors was greeted with one three-letter word: "Wow."

"I mean, look at that video board. Look at the LED lights, the incredible green grass, this incredibly orange clay," raved former Braves great Chipper Jones on Opening Day at SunTrust Park. "They watch how balls fly out of here and they see the skyline and everything, and they say, 'Wow.' I said it. Everybody else is going to say it. This is very impressive."

That goes to show that when it comes to the modern-day sports experience, size does not matter nearly as much as ambiance, convenience, proximity to the action and fun, forward thinking that puts the fan first. SunTrust Park seats just over 41,000 fans—down from the 50,000-seat capacity of Turner Field. Those fans, however, have options that dwarf those at most other parks in the country.

Children can enjoy a rock climbing wall in an area of the park that also includes a zip line. Grown-ups can watch the game and socialize at the three-story Chop House bar, where one of the craft beers available has been aged with actual wood from Mizuno baseball bats. Those

with a taste for art can eye some 300 pieces of Braves-themed art around the stadium, including a statue of former manager Bobby Cox and a magnificent, nine-foot photo of Hank Aaron hitting his then-record-breaking 715th career home run.

Need to find the nearest restroom or a particular item of food that's calling out to your palette? Just check your smart phone app.

"I'd like to welcome you to baseball's newest gem," major league commissioner Rob Manfred told fans on Opening Day—a crowd that included Jones, Cox, Aaron, Tom Glavine, Dale Murphy, Phil Niekro, John Smoltz and former President Jimmy Carter.

The Braves played at Atlanta-Fulton County Stadium from 1966-96 before moving to downtown Turner Field, where they won 100 or more games in five of their first seven seasons. However, Braves president John Schuerholz announced in 2013 that the team would be relocating, citing "hundreds of millions of dollars" in needed renovations to Turner Field.

Around the same time, city money was being funneled toward a downtown stadium for the city's NFL and MLS teams. The result was Mercedes Benz Stadium, which opened in 2017. Thus, the Braves looked outside of town, and—thanks largely to about $400 million in supporting public funds—wound up with a solution that resulted in

Cobb County hosting not only the team, but a unique surrounding area that was still growing as the Braves were getting used to their new stadium.

SunTrust Park is located within a neighborhood called The Battery. The Braves tout it as "the first of its kind—a destination that will simultaneously build and integrate a state-of-the-art Major League Baseball ballpark with a multi-use development and community." It features housing, restaurants, retail stores and a 4,000-seat live music venue—plenty to keep fans entertained before or after ballgames.

"The secret sauce of what's going on here is the synergy between The Battery and SunTrust Park," Braves chairman and CEO Terry McGuirk said midway through the team's first season at SunTrust, with attendance up about 37 percent compared with that point during their final year at Turner Field. "We think it has succeeded brilliantly."

It's once fans are inside the park, though, that the fun truly begins. The right field corner of the venue is a party from start to finish, with rooftop cabanas featuring ping-pong tables, foosball and other games, along with a Waffle House restaurant.

The cost of the entire project, including The Battery, is estimated to have topped $1 billion. Based on early reviews, the fans seem to be getting their money's worth from a trip to the park.

"It's a lot more intimate," Braves first baseman Freddie Freeman said, comparing SunTrust Park to Turner Field. "When you're out there playing, it feels like the fans are kind of right on you,

which at Turner Field, it was more relaxed. They were pushed back a little bit more. It's going to be a better experience for the fans and obviously for us, too."

Asked to name his favorite feature of the new park, Freeman did not hesitate. "375 to right-center," he said. The wall in that power alley is 15 feet closer to home plate than it was at Turner Field. Other than that, the dimensions are similar, so time will tell if SunTrust develops a reputation as a pitcher's park—like Turner Field was—or a hitter's haven like Fulton County Stadium. Chances are the numbers will place it somewhere in between.

In terms of fan experience, there is nothing "in between" about SunTrust. Lead designer Joe Spear said baseball has

been very responsive in addressing the things patrons want—great sightlines, food and beverage options, and opportunities to enjoy a game even when out of their seats.

To the latter end, SunTrust features several gathering spaces where fans can socialize while taking in the action. The Xfinity Rooftop above right field, the Hank Aaron Terrace in left, the Home Depot Clubhouse beyond left-center and the State Farm Deck below the main video board join the Chop House as hot spots for that purpose. "Below the Chop" puts fans almost in the right fielder's back pocket.

"You can have a conversation with the right fielder," Spear said. "He's going to be right there. You can hassle him if you want or cheer him if you want."

Above: Every seat in the house offers a fantastic view of the game. And anywhere a fan might wander away from that seat, he or she will find tastes of southern hospitality ranging from the iconic Chop House to a kid-friendly area that includes zip-lining and other fun activities.